PAGE STREET
PUBLISHING CO.

Distributed by Macmillan; sales in Canada by The Canadian Manda Group

22 21 20 19 18   1 2 3 4 5

ISBN-13: 978-1-62414-684-8
ISBN-10: 1-62414-684-8

Library of Congress Control Number: 2018945563

Cover and book design by Page Street Publishing Co.
Photography by Stacey Cramp

Printed and bound in China

THE BEST COMFORT FOOD ON THE PLANET

KERRY ALTIERO

CHEF/OWNER OF CAFE MIRANDA IN ROCKLAND, MAINE

WITH KATHERINE GAUDET

PHOTOGRAPHS BY STACEY CRAMP

PAGE STREET
PUBLISHING CO.

CAFE Miranda

DAILY LUNCH & SUPPER — SUNDAY BRUNCH

BECAUSE WE CAN
ESTD 1993
ROCKLAND MAINE

CONTENTS

FOREWORD

I met Kerry Altiero over fifteen years ago. I started visiting the midcoast area sometime in the 1990s, back when Rockland was full of empty storefronts. One night my uncle, a boat captain who lived in Camden at the time, asked me to join him for dinner at Cafe Miranda. What a surprise to stumble upon this gem of a café tucked on a little side street off the main drag. I still remember that I had local mussels, which were fabulous, great wood-fired bread and vegetables.

To me, Cafe Miranda is what a restaurant should be: a warm, comfortable atmosphere, good food, a welcoming host and a place where you can hang out like you are at your aunt's kitchen table. Part of the allure is the tiny open kitchen with a beautiful brick oven, tons of ingredients and an octopus-like chef wielding pans, plates and bowls, as happy as a kid in a candy shop. The menu is huge and very eclectic, including cuisine from around the world. There always seems to be something for everyone. It is sometimes daunting, but never disappointing. My favorites have always been Kerry's Italian dishes, the food he grew up with: handmade pasta, good pecorino, sausage and greens! Simple and delicious. There is also a good amount of silliness at Cafe Miranda, from the Elvis-inspired bathrooms to the menu descriptions, keeping it all fun and lighthearted.

When I decided to move to Rockland and open a restaurant, Kerry was one of the most welcoming people I met. He generously shared farmer information, codes, local scoop. A friendship was born. We have since cooked together for many local charities, culinary events and our local soup kitchen. We have become neighbors and comrades. It has been a wonderful thing to watch Kerry grow and continue to push the limits with his ever-growing menus. And the community has come together to support Kerry in the face of adversity. I saw this after a terrible fire at the restaurant in 2007. Cafe Miranda came back stronger than ever.

Kerry has been a supporter of the local farming community and local businesses, and a role model to many of the local kids who pass through his kitchen or dining room, or who benefit from a cooking class he teaches. He's fun, he's approachable and very real. Down to earth. I have learned a tremendous amount from watching him, listening to him. He has passion, fire that you do not come across every day, and he inspires not only his staff but his guests as well. This book lets him share all of his stories and passion with us all.

When Kerry asked me to write the foreword for his book, I was flattered. I have looked up to him as the pioneer chef of Maine. He took many chances and pushed boundaries that no one else was willing to do. He taught the locals about a different kind of dining scene and he won over their trust, paving the way for chefs like myself and many others who now have turned the midcoast into a food destination. Maine has always been a bounty of great ingredients—wild food, hippie foragers, small farmers, struggling dairy farms, fabulous seafood. It is a culinary oasis that was tapped by Kerry.

Maine is a very rich and a very poor state: rich with a bounty of amazing ingredients to work with, rich with people from all walks of life comingling together, farmers, fishermen, lobstermen, scallop divers, foragers all mixed in with summer folks, camp kids, artists, writers. However, it is not an easy place in which to make a living. The business is extremely seasonal; it's sometimes hard to find help. The winters can be brutal. When the summer is the only time you can do well, you don't get to relax and enjoy it. It's a place that calls for ingenuity. You can see some of that find-a-way spirit in these recipes, where ingredients and techniques are combined in unexpected ways to create new and wonderful tastes.

Kerry has always inspired me through his perseverance, his passion, his talent—but mostly by his genuinely giant heart. While sipping tea with him at Rock City Coffee in the middle of a blizzard one day, I saw each person who came in tap him on the back and give him a warm smile or an embrace. He is well loved in this community because he has been the mortar to hold it together through good times and bad. He pushes the limits, tries new ventures and continues to reinvent to please his guests. And he is still cooking. Happily cooking.

As I took a peek into this wonderful book, I knew it would become one of those books that does not collect dust, but becomes tattered and splashed with olive oil, tomato sauce and love. To read the history of how each dish got put on the menu and why some have never come off of it is just as much fun as the recipes. It is a life's work, not an easy life, but a life dedicated to cooking for others. Kerry aptly named the book *The Best Comfort Food on the Planet*. Comfort is what I feel when I sit at his table: warm, welcome and satiated.

Kerry is rock and roll. He's one of those badass cooks you want on your side when you're in the weeds. He loves what he does and this permeates every cell in his body, and every page of this book. I invite you to sink into this delicious treasure and let your inner rock and roll come out. Cook with gusto like Kerry and I am sure you will have happy bellies and lots of laughs!

Melissa Kelly

Melissa Kelly is the chef and owner of Primo restaurant in Rockland, Maine. In 2013 Melissa became the first two-time winner of the James Beard Best Chef: Northeast award.

INTRODUCTION

Two decades ago I started Cafe Miranda in a Maine fishing village. We offer a huge menu that mixes traditional American fare with Italian, Mexican, Middle Eastern, Thai, vegan . . . whatever strikes our fancy. Our motto is "Because We Can." We serve wonderful, surprising, innovative food that defies expectations and wins over all kinds of eaters. This cookbook will help you do the same at home, whether you are cooking for world-weary sophisticates or picky toddlers. Your kitchen may never be the same.

I've always had what you might call a contrary streak. In our little town of 7,000 residents, restaurants were traditionally built around deep fryers. We built ours around a wood-fire oven instead. It's great for bread and pizza, of course, but almost everything else goes in there, too: vegetables, casseroles and soups—almost everything benefits from a dose of high heat. Your home oven, cranked up, can create the same effect, while leaving your stovetop and your hands free for other things.

I admit to having some punkish tendencies. I like to do things my own way; I like speed; I like gears and metal. I'm addicted to the pace of restaurant cooking. But there are other, better reasons for seeking out adventures in food. Food can make the world bigger. It can change lives. For me it started in the '70s, touring around racing my motorcycle. I was a vegetarian then. Eating pinto beans with melted cheese and tortilla chips in every town got boring, so I learned to look abroad: to India and China and Mexico. All of this exploring gave me some great recipe ideas.

When I was just a motorcycle-racing kid from a coal town in Pennsylvania, food opened up the world for me. I want to include everyone in that experience, from New York foodies to local fishermen. The food you'll find in this book is gutsy, but it isn't strange for the sake of being strange. There is a lot that's familiar, comfortable enough to open the gate to new experiences.

Time and time again, I've seen limited eaters become adventurous ones. Jim Hall, who provides the wood for our oven, ate only spaghetti and meatballs for a very long time. One day he tried the Bolognese. Then he tried other things: the Mexican, the Thai. Now, when Jim travels, he likes to call and tell me what new crazy thing he's eating (and how much he's getting charged for it). Making people comfortable, serving real, bold food that isn't churned out by the industrial circus, getting fresh products into the mouths of the people we care about: These things change lives.

What these recipes do is modern but not new. They build on tradition and find new paths. When we opened in the early 1990s, our food looked strange to Mainers who were used to bread and butter on the tables and a choice of rice or baked potato with every entrée. Still, they recognized something in our food. The passion and the heart that we cook with comes out on the plate. You can't fake it. The Mainers who became our first customers understood that there was integrity and quality in the food even if they had no idea what it was.

We've been here over twenty years now, and have seen the town grow from a down-on-its-luck fishing village to a culturally rich tourist destination. It's the rare place where an influx of galleries and terrific restaurants hasn't erased the local character. It's a privilege to cook where you can operate in a way that focuses on integrity and honesty. That's what this cookbook tries to give you: delicious, real recipes you can make at home, with fresh ingredients, and without more than an average risk of fire damage. Crank up your oven, get yourself some good pot holders and let's get cooking.

1

STARTERS

The start of a meal is a wonderful thing. It's when you leave the rest of your day behind and tuck in for an evening of food, drink and conversation. The recipes in this chapter are about that glow of anticipation. They are built on strong, bright flavors and surprising combinations, unique enough to be conversation pieces themselves. You'll find the beginnings of all kinds of evenings in these pages. The Warm Zucchini Antipasto requires only the gentlest poaching of zucchini and bit of tomato chopping to start off a graceful summer meal; I Dreamt of Jerry is a spicy, meaty bowl to shovel in at the end of a long day. Try the Thai-spiced flavor bomb we call Beef Groce, the samosa-like Wontons from Spaaaace, the Mexican-inspired stuffed peppers of I Had It in Biddeford and the Middle Eastern lamb patties of Sorta Kefta. The best part is, this is just the beginning.

WARM ZUCCHINI ANTIPASTO

This recipe emerged from an off-the-menu request: A diner wanted a warm antipasto. Antonio Cassasanto, my boss at the Swallows in Cape May, came up with this simple, perfect dish. It blew me away then and it still does more than 30 years (and a lot of brain cells) later.

SERVES 2

---

1 decent-size zucchini

1 ripe tomato

Coarse salt

6 tbsp/90 ml extra-virgin olive oil (a good fruity one)

Coarsely ground black pepper

Cut the zucchini into quarters from tip to stem, giving you long strips with a cross-section that looks like a pie slice. Cut the tomato into ½-inch/1.5 cm slices.

Put about an inch/2.5 cm of water in a shallow 12-inch/30 cm nonreactive pan, add a good pinch of salt and bring it to a boil. Reduce the heat so that the water is simmering.

While the water is heating, place the slices of tomato on a plate and lightly salt them.

Poach the zuke in the simmering water until just barely cooked through. This will take about 5 minutes, but will depend on the size of your slices. The color will intensify; it should be bright, not drab.

Place the poached and warm zukes on top of the tomatoes. Drizzle with the olive oil. Grind the pepper over it.

Enjoy this with Prosecco and a pal: a fine start to a genteel evening.

RED CURRY MUSSELS

The first time I had this dish, when I was working at the Bayberry Inn in Cape May, my boss, Joe Lotozo, said, "If you ever have mussels that are better than this, you gotta tell me." I've never had to tell him. The salt in the fish sauce rips open your taste buds, and the curry flavor rushes in like soldiers when the line breaks. The herbs are fresh and aromatic and the coconut smooths everything out. Mussels are usually pretty good, but in this preparation they are spectacular.

SERVES 2

12 oz/355 ml coconut milk

2 tbsp/29 g red curry paste (preferably Maesri brand)

1 lb/454 g mussels, cleaned and debearded

5 basil leaves, Thai if you have it, or a combination of mint and basil

8 sprigs cilantro

1 lime

1 tbsp/15 ml Thai fish sauce, or to taste

Some rice or bread for dipping (optional)

Grab a large, heavy-bottomed, nonreactive saucepan. First, render some coconut fat: Put 3 tablespoons/45 ml of the coconut milk in the pan. Boil on medium-high heat until the milk stops bubbling, but before it starts smoking; this will only take a minute. Add the curry paste and stir vigorously so that it cooks in the fat briefly; don't brown it. Add the rest of the coconut milk and whisk for 20 seconds or so, until the liquid is an even, deep red. Taste and add more curry paste if you want it spicier.

Add the mussels to the pan and cover. Cook for 5 to 8 minutes, occasionally giving them a gentle stir. When most of the mussels have opened, add the basil and stir gently. Let sit for 1 minute, or until you can smell it. Remove from the heat and garnish with the cilantro. Squeeze the lime over the mussels and squirt with plenty of fish sauce. Serve with rice or with bread for dipping.

CHEF'S TIP: Look for green-lipped mussels for this dish, if you can't find Maine mussels. The best are three years old or less. How can you tell? Mussels grow rings every year, like trees, so you can look at the shell and see how many there are. Generally rope-grown mussels are freer of grit. If your mussels are wild or you just want to be safe, purge them first. Cover the shells with cold salted water and add a half-handful of cornmeal. Give it a stir every once in a while. After a couple of hours, the mussels will have eaten the cornmeal and spit out the sand.

FBOM (FABULOUS BOWL OF MEAT)

Like many people who work in kitchens, I occasionally employ the F-Bomb. But believe it or not, the Fabulous Bowl of Meat was on the menu for years before someone pointed out to me that the acronym has another meaning when you say it out loud. As a person who also occasionally likes a pun, I can say that this dish has no need for any extra salt or spice in the name (but hey, it doesn't hurt). It's an ideal appetizer: light, but hearty and super flavorful.

SERVES 2

1 ball cellophane mung bean thread or rice vermicelli noodles (about 1 oz/28 g dried noodles)

4 tbsp/60 ml vegetable oil

½ Spanish or yellow onion, cut into small dice

2 tbsp/29 g green curry paste (Maesri brand preferred)

1 lb/454 g ground turkey (you can also use ground pork or chicken)

2 to 4 tsp/10 to 20 ml Thai fish sauce

10 big leaves romaine lettuce, washed and dried

2 tbsp/8 g carrot, shredded

¼ cup/33 g red onion, sliced

5 sprigs cilantro

½ lime, cut into wedges

Soak the noodles in cold water until flexible, overnight if possible.

Heat the oil in a 12-inch/30 cm nonreactive skillet over medium heat. Add the Spanish onion and cook slowly until translucent, about 10 minutes. Add the curry paste and sauté for 5 minutes, until it smells really good. Add the ground turkey. As the meat cooks, break it up with a potato masher to keep it crumbled. When all the pink is gone, 5 to 8 minutes, remove from the heat and sprinkle with the fish sauce.

Break off the outer leaves of the romaine (keep the core for another purpose). Fan out the leaves in a nice, big, flat-bottomed bowl with shallow sides. You can use a plate; you'll have to change the name of the recipe, though. Place the carrot, red onion, cilantro, lime and rice noodles in piles around the perimeter of the bowl, and put the meat in the middle.

To eat, take a leaf and top it with a bit of everything and a squeeze of lime. Tilt your head in a taco-eating kind of way, and enjoy!

CHEF'S TIP: As with all curry dishes, the curry paste you use matters. The more standard supermarket brands will not give you the powerful, exciting flavor of a good Thai paste. It's worth seeking out the Maesri brand or another high-quality paste (probably featuring a Thai grandmother and no English on the label except the nutrition facts), which you can find in a specialty or Asian market or on the Internet. An extra stop or a Web order might be a little more trouble than going to the supermarket, but certainly easier than making your own curry!

BLUE APPLE APPETIZER

This simple, quick appetizer is the perfect combination of sweet, soft roasted apples, a rich blue cheese cream and fresh green chard. We use the apples from the old trees in the yard at Headacre Farm and the fantastic cider vinegar from Sewall Orchard, one of the oldest organic orchards around. Heirloom apples and quality vinegar will up the impact of this dish, but you can make this with your supermarket varieties, too. For the blue cheese, go ahead and use the cheap crumbles and save the better stuff for a cheese plate.

SERVES 2

2 apples

Olive oil

6 leaves chard, destemmed

1 cup minus 2 tbsp/236 ml heavy cream

4 oz/113 g blue cheese crumbles

2 leaves sage

1 tbsp/15 ml cider vinegar

Coarsely ground black pepper

Focaccia (page 159) or a good crusty bread

Preheat your oven to 375°F/191°C.

Halve and core the apples. Neat tip: Use a melon baller to scoop out the core. Brush them with olive oil. Place the apples in a 9½-inch/24 cm oven-safe casserole dish.

Toss the chard with a little oil and set aside.

Roast the apples until they just start to puff up, 20 to 30 minutes.

Add the cream and cheese; return to the oven. Bake until the sauce will coat a spoon, 5 minutes or so. Add the sage and chard. Continue to cook for a few minutes, until the chard is wilted. Remove from the oven. Drizzle with the vinegar. Grind lots of black pepper over. Wa-la.

Serve with bread to squeegee up all that great sauce. A fave wine pairing from back in the day is Honig Sauvignon Blanc. A perfect "pear."

LOBSTER ON A SHINGLE

The inspiration for this dish began in my Catholic grade school cafeteria. No, they did not serve us lobster. It was something else on a shingle. Many of you may remember the classic diner (and military) dish "Creamed Chipped Beef on Toast." We won't be impersonating that one, but using the idea and turning it into something fabulous. So, here in the Lobster Capital of the World, we make a creamed lobster with tomato, tarragon and wilted greens and serve it over toasted focaccia.

SERVES 2

4 (7" x 2"/18 x 5 cm) strips of Focaccia (page 159) or other substantial bread

6 tbsp/90 ml extra-virgin olive oil

2 cups/473 ml heavy cream (36% or more fat)

½ tsp fresh garlic, minced

2 tbsp/30 ml fortified wine (dry marsala is good)

½ cup/80 g ripe tomatoes, diced

5 oz/142 g cooked lobster meat, cut into large dice

¼ cup/57 g Romano or Parmesan cheese, grated

4 cups/120 g spinach, stemmed if necessary

1 sprig tarragon

Coarse salt

Coarsely ground black pepper

Brush the bread with some of the olive oil and toast in a 350°F/177°C oven, 8 to 10 minutes. It should be golden brown, like toast.

Place the cream, garlic, wine and tomatoes in a 12-inch/30 cm heavy-bottomed, nonreactive pan. On medium heat, simmer to reduce and thicken the cream mixture. (It's fine to boil cream, and it will thicken. This won't work with milk.) Your goal is to end up with about half the volume of the liquid that you started with, which will take 8 minutes or so, depending on how much liquid is in your tomatoes. You are looking for the coat-a-spoon consistency.

Remove the cream mixture from the heat and add the lobster, cheese, spinach and tarragon. Cover. This will warm the lobster, melt the cheese and wilt the greens. Adjust the seasoning with salt and pepper.

On a platter or 2 plates, arrange the focaccia strips at the 4 "corners." Pour the lobster mixture in the center. Drizzle with the remaining olive oil and sprinkle with pepper.

BRUNCH VARIATION: Poach 4 eggs and place 2 on each plate, on top of the lobster and toast.

CHEF'S TIP: I highly recommend buying cooked fresh lobster meat. The price is well worth it, when you consider the time and effort that goes into picking a lobster. If you are picking your own, you'll get about 3 ounces/85 g of meat from your average 1½-pound/680 g lobster.

50 MPH TOMATOES

You know how people think Chicago is called the Windy City because it's windy, but it was originally called that because the politicians talked so much? Something similar happened with 50 MPH Tomatoes; this is an extra-zippy dish, and it does fly off the plates, but the name has another origin. A lot of the tomatoes you can get in the winter (and year-round in most supermarkets) have to withstand highway speeds, and so are pretty hard and not as flavorful as we'd wish. This recipe takes advantage of winter tomatoes' firmness, which makes them ideal for frying, and amps up the flavor with a variation on our "Ranch" dressing. They are spicy, crispy and juicy and in demand year-round.

SERVES 1 TO 2

50 MPH DRESSING
½ cup/110 g mayonnaise
1 tbsp/15 g hot pepper relish
2 tsp/10 g sweet relish
½ tsp paprika
Sprinkle cayenne pepper
Coarsely ground black pepper
2 tsp/4 g dried onion or minced fresh onion
2 pinches dried dill

½ cup/85 g cornmeal
Pinch salt
A few grinds black pepper
½ lb/227 g tomatoes, cut into 1"/2.5 cm slices
Vegetable oil, for frying
Scallions, sliced

Mix the dressing ingredients together in a bowl and set aside.

Combine the cornmeal with the salt and pepper in a bowl. Then coat the tomato slices in the mixture.

In a heavy 12-inch/30 cm stainless-steel or cast-iron skillet over medium heat, heat ¼ inch/6 mm of oil; don't let it smoke. Fry the tomatoes for 5 minutes, until golden brown, then flip them and fry until golden on the other side, another 5 minutes. Drain on paper towels.

Smear some dressing on a plate. Don't stack the tomatoes; plate them side by side so that crust you have created so carefully doesn't turn to mush. Sprinkle with scallions and serve.

BEEF GROCE

This dish is as irresistible and addictive as it is hard to categorize. I created it when Susan Groce—artist, professor, violinist and kick-ass cook, among other things—asked me for a low-starch, low-fat, summery and very spicy dish. This dish is all of those things, and so much more. It's a hearty salad of mixed greens and cellophane noodles, with a dressing full of big Thai-inspired flavors and a scattering of beef that's fried until crunchy. It's a true Miranda classic, just like its namesake.

SERVES 1 TO 2

¼ cup/33 g red onion, sliced thinly

2 cups/60 g mixed salad greens, such as mesclun

¼ cup/20 g radicchio, shredded

1 tbsp/10 g cooked unsalted peanuts, chopped

1 tbsp/4 g carrot, shredded

3 tbsp plus 1 tsp/50 ml sambal oelek

1 tbsp/15 ml Thai fish sauce

2 tbsp/30 ml freshly squeezed lime juice

¼ cup/44 g cellophane mung bean thread or rice vermicelli noodles, soaked according to package directions

6 leaves basil

3 tbsp/45 ml vegetable oil

3 oz/85 g shaved steak, chopped into 1"/2.5 cm pieces

4 sprigs cilantro

In a medium bowl, place all the ingredients, except the oil, beef and cilantro.

Heat the oil in a wok or skillet and add the shaved steak. Stir-fry, breaking it up while frying. What you are doing is desiccating the beef, making it crispy, rendering what fat may be in it and flavoring the oil. (Beef-flavored oil! Forget the truffle oil, baby!) This may take 5 to 10 minutes. Get it brown and crispy! When it's there—that is, crispy (hear me yet?)—remove from the heat.

While hot, dump the contents of the wok into the bowl. Toss everything together, plate in an Asian-style bowl, top with the cilantro and serve with chopsticks.

Eat with beer, lots. A Geary's Pale Ale from Portland is a Maine classic and a good choice.

CHEF'S TIP: Sambal oelek (Thai chili-garlic sauce) is widely available in the ethnic aisles of supermarkets, even here in our little fishing village. You'll find the Thai fish sauce and noodles there, too.

GNOCCHI IN SAUCE ROSA

This is a big-time fave of anyone who has tried it. Soft, toothsome gnocchi in a pink, creamy sauce will bring comfort and warmth to any evening. I advise serving this in small portions as an appetizer; it is quite filling.

My recipe is a variation of the traditional potato item. I add more flour to give these Italian dumplings a chewier and more interesting texture. To get a more consistent result, we also use potato flakes.

MAKES 4 SERVINGS

GNOCCHI

¾ lb/340 g boiled russet potatoes, peeled and well mashed, or prepared potato flakes (about 1⅔ cups/140 g), at room temperature

1 lb/454 g all-purpose flour

2 large egg yolks

2 tbsp/22 g Parmesan cheese, grated

1 tbsp/2 g fresh parsley, minced

Salt

Coarsely ground black pepper

SAUCE

3 cups/612 ml Latex Marinara (page 218)

2 cups/444 ml heavy cream

½ cup/112 ml dry marsala wine

8 leaves basil

To make the gnocchi, mix all the ingredients together to form a dough. If it's too wet to handle, you can add more flour, but keep it as wet as you can. Turn onto a lightly floured board. Shape the mixture into a rope ¾ inch/2 cm in diameter (remember your Play-Doh days?). Cut it into 1-inch/2.5 cm sections. Push your thumb into each to make an indentation in the center. You want it to be about the same thickness all the way through, and you don't want it too thick or you'll end up with lead balloons instead of potato pillows.

Boil a pot of water and cook the gnocchi until they float and are consistently textured throughout. This can take from 5 to 15 minutes, so check on them a few times. Drain and toss in olive oil. You should have 2 cups/240 g of cooked gnocchi.

To make the sauce, place all but the basil in a 12-inch/30 cm nonreactive sauté pan over medium heat. Simmer, stirring occasionally. The sauce should reduce to a coat-a-spoon thickness in about 8 minutes. When it is ready, the bubbles will be popping rather than rolling. Add the basil and cook for 1 minute more.

Add the gnocchi to the pan of sauce. Toss together, then spoon out onto a heated plate.

> **CHEF'S TIP:** I recommend making a big batch of gnocchi, and freezing some of it parcooked. Remove the gnocchi from the boiling water when they are half-cooked, and shock in cold running water, keeping the water running until the gnocchi are cool. Spread them out on a towel on a cookie sheet to get rid of some of the moisture. Then transfer to a dry cookie sheet to freeze. Once frozen, transfer to a plastic bag. When you are ready to use the gnocchi, put your sauce ingredients in the pan and add the gnocchi. They will heat through in the time it takes your sauce to come together.

I HAD IT IN BIDDEFORD

This is a riff on a dish I had at Los Tapatios, a great hole-in-the-wall in a southern Maine mill town. It is actually in a basement rather than a hole in a wall, and serves terrific, un-fancy Mexican fare. Our version of this one consists of roasted peppers stuffed with potato and fresh cheese, finished with Sauce El Camino. I highly recommend making this dish with your leftover Thanksgiving mashed potatoes for a total, delicious change of pace.

This is a starter, but you can turn it into a fine vegetarian entrée by adding a cup each of Black Bean Ragout (page 212) and The Usual Suspects (page 101).

SERVES 2

---

1 cup/210 g Garlic Mashed Potatoes (page 107)

⅓ cup/82 g queso fresco or ricotta cheese

2 poblano peppers, cut tip to stem and seeded

½ cup/60 g bread crumbs

1 tbsp/15 ml vegetable oil

1½ cups/355 ml Sauce El Camino (page 216), warmed

1 tbsp/14 g black sesame seeds

5 sprigs cilantro

2 lime quarters

Preheat your oven to 375°F/191°C, or fire up a smoker.

Fold the cheese into the mashed potatoes. Fill the peppers with the mixture and top with the bread crumbs. Drizzle with a bit of oil to moisten the crumbs. Arrange them in a 9-inch/23 cm oven-safe casserole dish. Splash a little water, about ⅛ inch/3 mm deep, into your pan. You want the peppers to cook through without browning too much. Put in the oven or smoker.

Roast until the skin of the peppers starts to brown, around 45 minutes. You want the peppers and potato mix to be heated through and well browned. Add more water if they seem to be charring rather than cooking.

Spread the warmed Sauce El Camino on a warmed platter; smear it around. Top with the peppers, sprinkle with the sesame seeds, throw the cilantro on top and squeeze the lime over all.

I can see Dave Geary eating this with one of his fine Pale Ales. OK, two.

SORTA KEFTA

This dish borrows from the many lamb-eating cultures of the Middle East, the Mediterranean and North Africa. The spiced patties of lamb are served with fresh, cool vegetables and yogurt and sprinkled with our magical Secret Spice. It's fun to make and delightful to eat.

SERVES 2

PATTIES

14 oz/497 g ground lamb

¼ tsp cumin seeds, toasted

¾ cup/60 g fresh parsley, chopped

2 tbsp/18 g garlic, minced

Salt

FOR ASSEMBLY

½ cup/80 g tomato, diced, tossed in olive oil and sprinkled with salt

6 tbsp/90 g plain yogurt

¼ cup/30 g cucumber, shredded (I like to shred this on a mandoline)

1½ cups/45 g spinach, stemmed if necessary

¾ tsp Secret Spice (page 224)

1 tsp black sesame seeds

½ lemon

2 tbsp/30 ml extra-virgin olive oil

Salt

Warm a platter. Heat your trusty 8-inch/20 cm (or larger) cast-iron skillet over medium-high heat.

Mix the patty ingredients together and shape into 4 equal patties, 1 inch/2.5 cm thick. Place the patties in the skillet and cook to medium-rare, 5 minutes or so, flipping once.

On the platter, place in separate piles: tomato, yogurt, cukes, lamb patties.

Toss the spinach in the pan and wilt, just for a minute. Add it to the plate.

Sprinkle with the Secret Spice and black sesame seeds. Squeeze the lemon around. Drizzle the olive oil. Sprinkle with salt (go heavy over the spinach).

SEARED SCALLOPS IN ASIAN BROTH

Scallops have to be one of the world's great high-end proteins. OK, yes, I say this about tuna, lobster, crab . . . but it's all true. Searing a scallop on a cast-iron pan makes a sweet (like sugar, not like a figure of speech from a ski bum) caramelized coating that is, well, pretty sweet. Serving these in a broth spiced with Thai flavors is downright elegant.

SERVES 1

3 oz/85 g dry Maine sea scallops

Olive oil

½ cup/118 ml fish fumet, fish stock or canned clam juice (choose a natural, low-salt clam juice)

2 tbsp/28 g bamboo shoots marinated in chili oil (available at Asian markets)

4 leaves Thai basil

2 scallions, sliced on the bias

Lemon wedge

Heat your 9-inch/23 cm cast-iron pan on high heat.

Oil the scallops just to coat and place on the skillet. Let the first side brown well. The aroma is intoxicating! The scallops' interiors should stay cool to the touch. Do not flip them. Just get that brown caramelization thing happening and remove from the heat. It should take 4 minutes or so.

In a 3-quart/3 L nonreactive saucepan, warm the fumet to just short of boiling. Then remove the saucepan full of fumet from the heat and add the bamboo shoots and basil. Turn out this mixture into an Asian-style bowl (like the ones used for pho or donburi). Place the scallops seared side up on top of the mixture. Sprinkle with the scallions. Squeeze the lemon over and toss the wedge into the bowl.

Serve with a flat-bottomed Asian soupspoon and a pair of chopsticks.

CHEF'S TIP: Look for "dry" scallops. The best are "diver" scallops, fetched from King Neptune's locker by a person in scuba gear. These are great just as they come. Squeeze a lime, salt one and eat it raw. Second choice is "day boat." Just as it sounds: The fishermen come in every night to land the catch, so you can buy it fresh. After that comes "dragger" scallops, which are perfectly acceptable as long as they are "dry." This has nothing to do with their wit or humor, more with processing. It means they haven't been soaked in water, brine or chemicals that plump them up and add to their weight. The liquid makes it difficult, if not impossible, to sear them. So check with your fishmonger, and call them on it if your "dry" scallops start bleeding water. And yes, those "individually quick frozen" ones fall into the "wet" category.

BULB OF GARLIC APPETIZER

This is an interactive dish that you disassemble, reassemble and chat over during a leisurely repast. It's fun. (That, or a pain in the ass.) The creamy sweet mellowness of whole roasted garlic is unexpected and quite satisfying. Make a lot; you will love it.

You can do the base prep days in advance and finish as you wish.

SERVES 1

---

1 whole bulb garlic (the bigger the cloves, the easier it will be to pick 'em outta there)

½ bay leaf

Olive oil

Salt and coarsely ground black pepper

1 sprig thyme

¼ cup/60 ml brown stock

1½ oz/42 g blue cheese

1½ tbsp/23 ml marsala wine

¼ cup/60 ml heavy cream

½ cup/30 g spinach or other mild greens, stemmed, tossed in oil

Focaccia (page 159), to serve

Preheat your oven to 350°F/177°C.

Lay the garlic on its side on a bench or cutting board. Use a sharp knife to slice off the top (that would be the opposite of the root end), just exposing the clove tips. You want to see ⅛ inch/3 mm of each clove.

In a 7-inch/18 cm oven-safe casserole dish, place the garlic on top of the bay leaf, root side down. Liberally brush the bulb with olive oil, taking special care to soak the insides of the parchmentlike skin between the cloves. Sprinkle all over with salt and pepper.

Roast for 30 to 45 minutes, or until the cloves are uniformly soft. The skin should be a bit brown, not black. If you see that it's getting dark, put a piece of foil over the garlic to protect it from the direct heat.

Proceed to the finished dish, or chill the bulb to use later.

Put the roasted bulb (warm or chilled) in a small oven-safe casserole dish and top with the thyme. Add the rest of the ingredients, except the spinach, to the pan.

Into the oven, loping along at 350°F/177°C. If your bulb was chilled, try 40 minutes. If not, 15 to 20 will do it. The sauce should reduce to a coat-a-spoon consistency. If you've used a metal casserole dish, you can transfer it to the stovetop and boil it down.

When the sauce has thickened and the bulb is hot throughout, pick up the bulb and put the spinach underneath. Return to the oven for a minute or two to wilt, not cook, the greens.

Serve hot in the casserole dish with a sharp white Bordeaux. Let it cool a bit, then use a lobster pick to extract the cloves or squeeze them onto the waiting focaccia.

USE THE GREEN PEPPERS

This one came about one day when I was planning to make myself a pizza at home on the farm. We happened to have a lot of peppers on hand and a pie seemed the right place for them until . . . I burned the pizza. Happens to all of us. The result was a delicious antipasto made from would-be pizza fixings: green peppers, feta, red onion, oregano and olives over focaccia croutons. What a delicious accident. If you have croutons already made, this requires no cooking, so it's perfect for a warm summer evening.

SERVES 2

---

2 large green bell peppers
½ cup/67 g oil- or salt-cured black olives
Leaves from 3 sprigs oregano
⅓ cup/44 g red onion, sliced thinly
½ cup/123 g feta cheese, crumbled
½ cup/118 ml extra-virgin olive oil
2 tsp/4 g coarsely ground black pepper
½ cup/40 g fresh parsley, chopped coarsely
Focaccia Croutons (page 213)

Seed the peppers and rip them by hand into 1½-inch/4 cm pieces. You will have about 2 loosely packed cups/300 g.

If you are using salt-cured olives, rinse and pat dry.

Toss all the ingredients, except the croutons, together in a bowl. You can serve right away, or let it marinate, tossing from time to time, until you are ready to eat.

Pile on a plate and arrange the croutons around the salad.

A round of ouzo, please.

WONTONS FROM SPAAAACE

These, I thought when I invented them, are like no other wonton on earth. They are large triangles filled with winter squash and flavored with our amazing Secret Spice, which is basically curry from heaven. Then, recently, I had an Indian samosa for the first time. So much for an original idea. The ingredients are different but the effect is similar: a crispy fried exterior around a soft, warm, spiced filling. So maybe they are not from space, but from the subcontinent by way of the Headacre Farm garden and my own crazy brain.

SERVES 6

1½ cups/210 g butternut squash, peeled, seeded and cut into large dice (from one average-size squash)

½ cup/66 g onion, sliced

2 cloves garlic

1 bay leaf

1 large egg

6 egg roll wrappers

½ cup/57 g Secret Spice (page 224)

Salt

Coarsely ground black pepper

1 cup/30 g spinach, stemmed and chopped

Vegetable oil, for frying

¼ cup/40 g ripe tomato, diced

½ seedless cucumber, shredded

1 cup/355 ml plain yogurt

2 tsp/9 g black sesame seeds

6 sprigs cilantro

2 lemon wedges

In a large saucepan, place the squash, onion, garlic and bay leaf. Add water until it covers the vegetables by an inch/2.5 cm. Bring to a boil over high heat, then lower the heat to a simmer. Cook, covered, until the squash is fork-tender. Drain and mash well, using a hand masher or an electric mixer. This can be coarse or smooth. Put in the refrigerator to chill.

Beat the egg together with a tablespoon/15 ml of water. Place the egg roll wrappers on the counter.

Mix the squash filling together with half of the Secret Spice and salt and pepper to taste. Divide it into 6 equal parts.

Place each piece of filling in the center of a wrapper. Distribute the spinach among the wrappers.

Brush a ¼-inch/6 mm-wide line of egg mixture around the border of each wrapper. Fold the wrapper point to point to make a triangle and press the edges to seal. Nudge the filling to distribute it a little, leaving a ¾-inch/2 cm border.

At this point, the wontons can be refrigerated for up to 2 days.

To cook, put 1 inch/2.5 cm of oil into a heavy pan over medium-high heat (or use a deep fryer set to 350°F/177°C). Fry until golden brown (in batches if needed). Drain on paper towels.

On a warm platter, arrange the tomato, cucumber and yogurt in small piles next to the wontons. Sprinkle with the sesame seeds and remaining Secret Spice and top with the cilantro. Squeeze the lemon over (you could just put the wedges on the plate, but you never can depend on folks to get the hint).

I like to sip a Maine Root Ginger Brew for a gingery addition to an exotic dish from SPAAAACE!

STUFFED MANGOES

These are not stuffed mangoes. They are really stuffed peppers, filled with risotto, caramelized onion and ricotta, served with marinara. The name comes from my Nanna, Connie Altiero. It wasn't just her; in the Pennsylvania Italian-American community where I grew up everyone called green peppers mangoes. I was seventeen before I entered a real supermarket (rather than the local Acme) and perused the amazing racks of produce. This was my initial encounter with a kiwi, a star fruit, and . . . a mango? *That isn't a mango, it's a fruit!* I don't recommend trying this recipe with any exotic fruits, but I do highly recommend it with green peppers. It's comfort food at its best.

SERVES 2

Olive oil

½ cup/66 g onion, sliced

2 large green bell peppers

8 medium button mushrooms, smashed

2 bay leaves

1 cup/170 g parcooked Risotto (page 109)

½ cup/124 g ricotta cheese

Salt

Coarsely ground black pepper

2 oz/57 g coarsely grated Romano cheese

2 cups/473 ml hot Latex Marinara (page 218)

Preheat your oven to 375°F/191°C. Place a 12-inch/30 cm sauté pan over medium heat and cover the bottom with a thin film of olive oil. Add the onion and sauté for about 10 minutes, stirring occasionally so that the onion caramelizes.

When the onion is brown and sweet smelling, add the mushrooms and bay leaves. Continue to sauté until the mushrooms are cooked through, another 3 to 5 minutes. Remove from the heat and chill (the vegetables, not you!).

In a suitable bowl, place the risotto, the mushroom sludge, salt and pepper and the cheeses. Mix it all together.

Slice the peppers in half from stem to tip. Try to leave the stem intact. Take out the seeds.

Brush the inside and outside of the peppers with olive oil and salt them. Divide the risotto mixture among the peppers. Place in a 9 x 12-inch/23 x 30 cm nonreactive metal roasting pan, stuffing side up. Roast until the stuffing is browned and the peppers are tender, which can take anywhere from 45 minutes to an hour and a half.

Spread the Latex Marinara on a warmed platter and put the peppers on top. You'll want to provide steak knives for cutting them up.

Chianti in the basket again, say you?

WAFFLE HOUSE FRIES

One of our longtime staffers, India, had worked at a waffle house as a teen and tipped us off to this idea: fries with brown gravy and two kinds of melted cheese. The sauce is the key. If you have a homemade brown veal or beef stock on hand, by all means, use that. Otherwise, choose a natural low- or no-salt beef broth for your gravy.

This is good as a starter, but it is really best eaten after a night on the town that involves karaoke and some forgotten details . . .

SERVES 2 TO 3

3 russet or other starchy potatoes

6 cups/1.4 L beef or veal stock

4 tbsp/57 g (½ stick) butter

½ cup plus 1 tbsp/56 g all-purpose flour

Canola oil, for frying

3 oz/85 g Cheddar cheese, shredded

2 oz/57 g mozzarella cheese, shredded

2 tbsp/10 g fresh parsley, coarsely chopped

Salt and pepper

Cut the potatoes into ½-inch/1.5 cm matchsticks and prepare according to the directions on page 110, up through the first cooking of the fries. Let them cool to room temperature.

Put the broth in a 2½- to 3-quart/2.5 to 3 L saucepan and boil to reduce by half. That would be 3 cups/710 ml, sailor. It may take 20 or 30 minutes, depending on your pan and your burner.

Place another 2½- to 3-quart/2.5 to 3 L saucepan over the lowest heat you can manage. Put in the butter and flour and cook, stirring, for about 15 minutes, until the raw flour taste is gone. This will make a roux to thicken the gravy.

Whisk the heated and reduced stock into the roux. It will thicken, magically. You can do this step days in advance, and if you make extra it's nice to have gravy on hand for other things. Keep the gravy hot while the fries cook.

Preheat your oven to 350°F/177°C.

Follow the directions on page 110 to cook the fries a second time.

Once the fries are cooked, toss them with everything else in an oven-safe bowl. Pop them into the oven to melt the cheese, about 8 minutes. Plate on a heated platter. Serve right now, as these do have a small window of optimal goodness.

Try it late at night with a couple of eggs "slimy and lookin' at ya" (sunny-side up and just set). Equally good with a Bloody Mary, a coffee or a Coke, depending on your needs.

JERRY FRIES

We have a whole series of "Jerry" dishes, as you'll see as you read through this book. They all involve the strange and magical combination of chili sauce and blue cheese. Given the psychedelic nature of this flavor, people tend to think it's named after Jerry Garcia, but in fact the inspiration was Jerry Brooks from Union, Maine. Back in Miranda's early days, Jerry waited tables for us after working at his physically demanding day job. At the end of the night, exhausted, he would sit at the counter with Sriracha, blue cheese and bread, shoveling the mess into his mouth with an expression that showed his brain was on pause. We took the hint and started inventing dishes that would actually nourish him. You might think that Thai spices and blue cheese have no business being together, but if you think of buffalo wings you'll get the idea.

SERVES 2 AS A SHARED APPETIZER

3 oz/85 g blue cheese, crumbled (use the cheap stuff)

½ cup/66 g red onion, sliced

6 tbsp/90 ml sweet chili sauce (we use Mae Ploy brand)

¼ cup/60 ml Sriracha

1 tbsp/15 ml Thai fish sauce

1 tbsp/10 g peanuts, chopped

3 large sweet potatoes, peeled and cut into ½"/1.5 cm thick fries

Vegetable oil, for frying

1 lime, halved

Heat your deep fryer (or a large, heavy saucepan of oil) to 325°F/163°C.

Mix everything but the potatoes, oil and lime in a large bowl.

Drop half of the potatoes into the oil. Cook until creamy inside and pleasantly brown outside, about 6 minutes per batch. Don't let them get too dark. Drain and drop into the bowl. Cook the other batch, drain, bowl. Toss gently. Squeeze the lime over. Serve at once, as these have a rather limited shelf life.

Jerry would have a Singha brewski with this.

I DREAMT OF JERRY

This one actually came to me in a dream. Jerry was sitting at our bar, and instead of his usual bread with blue cheese and Sriracha, he was eating a very oniony, garlicky burger with banana peppers. I could actually smell it in my sleep. I woke up and decided we needed to serve a deconstructed burger with the classic Jerry flavors of chili and blue cheese. It's the perfect thing to eat when you need charging up.

SERVES 1 AS A HEARTY APP

1 (8 oz/227 g) ground beef hamburger patty
½ cup/118 ml Jerry Dressing (page 62)
1 tbsp/10 g hot banana peppers, chopped
¼ cup/33 g red onion, sliced thinly
¼ cup/20 g fresh parsley, chopped coarsely
2 tbsp/30 ml extra-virgin olive oil
Coarsely ground black pepper

Heat a small skillet over medium-high heat. Cook the hamburger for 3 minutes on each side, until medium-rare. Try to get some char on it. You should reach an interior temperature of 135°F/57°C.

Break up the burger into a bowl. Add the rest of the stuff, except the black pepper, and toss. Top with a grind of black pepper and eat with good bread.

2

SOUPS AND SALADS

At Cafe Miranda, soups and salads aren't dainty little dishes for ladies who lunch (though they are always very popular on our lunch menu, with ladies and others). We take the same approach to these as we do to everything else: We make them big, flavorful and exciting.

The salads in this chapter are dinner-size and packed with all the good stuff we can get in there. What we don't do is the kind of anemic side salad that gets left on the plate. Some favorites are the Gnu Evan's (equal parts salad and French fries), Sally's Simple Salad (with raisins, ricotta salata and lots of arugula) and the Et Tu, Brutus? (which kills your average Caesar). Whether as meals by themselves or beside the other recipes in this book, these salads stand up for themselves.

Being located in a coastal town in Maine, we know the value of a good soup. Drizzly summers as well as frigid winters demand bowls that are hot, satisfying and exciting enough to perk up a dark week. At the same time, I don't want to have to keep a pot boiling on the stovetop all day long; I've got other uses for my stovetop and my days. So I've created recipes that come together quickly and easily, using the freezer and the oven as well as the range. Our bean soups are based on make-ahead bases that you can keep on hand in the freezer for nearly instant meals. We have chowders that roast in the oven, and Asian-style broths that hardly need cooking at all. It's all the comfort with none of the waiting!

BIG BACON UNIT

This is a take on the wilted (on purpose) salads from Pennsylvania Dutch restaurants I ate at in my youth. The BBU is fabulously flavorful, and definitely dinner-worthy on its own or with a hunk of bread.

If you can get bacon "ends," the by-product of those perfect shingled packs, they are great and usually waaaayy cheaper. Failing that, thick cut or slab is good.

SERVES 1

4 oz/113 g uncooked quality thick-cut bacon

3 cups/90 g mixed salad greens, preferably including more rugged varieties, such as baby kale, chard or spinach

¼ cup/40 g tomato, sliced

¼ cup/33 g red onion, sliced

4 tbsp/60 ml balsamic vinegar

1 clove garlic, minced

6 tbsp/90 ml extra-virgin olive oil

2 red potatoes, boiled and quartered

2 tbsp/22 g Romano or Parmesan cheese, coarsely grated

Cut the bacon into chunks about as big as your thumb from the last joint to the tip. Odd bits are OK, too.

Place the greens, tomato, onion, vinegar and garlic in a heat-resistant bowl (you are going to be pouring in hot oil, so don't use plastic).

In a 6-inch/15 cm skillet, on medium heat, place the bacon, potatoes and 4 tablespoons/60 ml of the olive oil. Sauté to crisp and render some of that delish fat out of the bacon. Browning the potatoes is OK but not necessary. When the bacon is crisped (not too much; we want it chewy, not brittle), in about 4 minutes, carefully pour the entire contents of the pan into the bowl of salad mixture. Toss your salad. Dish it out onto a plate and top with the cheese and the rest of the oil. Voilà!

Enjoy this with a Frye's Leap IPA from Sebago or powerful red wine.

HOT. DRESSED. SALAD.

This is what we call a "stealth vegetarian" dish. That is to say, meat eaters eat it happily, only later asking, "Hey, where was the beef?" It's more common to see hot-dressed salads made with bacon (see the Big Bacon Unit [page 37]), but here the hearty greens, mushroom and cheese bring so much flavor and body that bacon would be overkill.

You can replace the tatsoi with other heavier greens, such as kale, but not collard-like tough ones.

SERVES 2

3 cup/100 g loosely packed tatsoi, washed and shaken dry

⅓ cup/53 g tomato, chopped

1 tsp garlic, minced (about ⅔ clove)

3 tbsp/45 ml balsamic vinegar

½ cup/113 g olive oil (yes, half a cup!)

⅓ cup/44 g red onion, sliced

1 portobello mushroom, cut into ¾"/2 cm dice

⅓ cup/57 g Romano cheese, shaved

Focaccia (page 159), to serve

In a medium bowl, place the greens, tomato, garlic and balsamic.

Heat the oil to just short of smoking in a heavy 10-inch/25.5 cm or larger skillet or saucepan. Add the onion and mushroom and brown well, about 3 minutes. Remove from the heat.

Don your safety glasses. Gently, pouring away from you, pour the oil and cooked vegetables into the bowl with the greens. Toss with tongs. The greens will slightly wilt and the color will intensify.

Turn out onto a platter. Sprinkle with the cheese. Serve with focaccia or another good bread, vino, company.

SALLY'S SIMPLE SALAD

Many years ago Sally Fernald, one of our longtime customers, requested a salad that was more interesting than your basic garden variety but without any heavy dressing or rich ingredients that might fill you up before the meal starts. The result is this perfectly balanced salad: spicy arugula and crunchy radicchio with a simple lemon dressing, highlighted with pine nuts, raisins, cheese and a touch of fennel. It's great as a first course, next to a plate of spaghetti or on its own as a light lunch.

SERVES 2

4 cups/120 g young arugula
2 cups/113 g radicchio, shredded
¼ cup/33 g red onion, sliced finely
1 tbsp/8 g pine nuts, toasted
1 tsp garlic, minced finely
Juice of ½ lemon
1½ tbsp/15 g raisins
Pinch fennel seeds, toasted
¼ cup/60 ml extra-virgin olive oil
1½ oz/43 g ricotta salata

Toss all the ingredients together in a bowl. Enjoy!

ET TU, BRUTUS?

This recipe emerged at the Marquis de Lafayette Hotel in Cape May. The owner, an eccentric type, decided that he didn't like the usual Caesar salad dressing and that his chefs should compete to invent a new one. Now, I was the pastry chef. It wasn't really my area at the time. This was one of those cases where ignorance is an advantage. While all the real cooks were carefully whisking away with forks, I threw eggs, olive oil, garlic, Romano and basil (no anchovies) into a blender. I won. Caesar was dead.

SERVES 2 (WITH DRESSING LEFT OVER)

DRESSING

1 tbsp/11 g Romano cheese, grated

1 pasteurized egg yolk

4 leaves basil

¼ cup/60 ml vegetable oil

½ cup/120 ml extra-virgin olive oil

2 tsp/9 ml water

1 whole clove garlic

2½ tsp/12 ml freshly squeezed lemon juice

SALAD

⅔ head hearts of romaine lettuce, ripped into bite-size chunks

¼ red onion, sliced thinly

8 (1"/2.5 cm) chunks of fresh Focaccia (page 159) or other crusty bread

¼ cup/10 g radicchio, shredded

¼ cup/44 g Romano or Parmesan cheese, shredded

Coarsely ground black pepper

Roasted red peppers

Place all the dressing ingredients, except the oil, in your trusty food processor and spin until the mixture is pale. Slowly add the oil. You are making an emulsion, as you would for mayonnaise or hollandaise sauce, and if you add too much oil at once you'll get an oily, broken dressing. Once all the oil has been added, set aside.

Put the lettuce, onion, bread and radicchio in a large stainless-steel bowl. Add the dressing and toss. Plate, sprinkling with the Romano and ground pepper and arranging red peppers on top, where the anchovies usually go.

Mangia! And beware the Ides of March.

CHEF'S TIP: Pasteurized egg yolks are available in the frozen section of the grocery store. You can also use a yolk from a very fresh large egg—local and/or organic is safest.

GNU EVAN'S

This salad was invented as a desperate attempt to get my then-twelve-year-old son to eat salad (or anything other than bagels with cream cheese). It's a simple concept: mix equal parts salad and French fries.

The best way to make fries is a double deep-fry, as described on page 110. But there is a cheater method that involves the microwave, still makes delicious fries and is easier for casual dinners. The instructions are below.

SERVES 2

2 large russet potatoes, or 2 lb/907 g other starchy potatoes

Canola oil, for frying

4 to 6 cups/120 to 150 g mixed field greens (or an equal volume to the French fries)

¼ cup/33 g red onion, sliced

3 tbsp/45 ml good olive oil

¼ lemon

¼ cup/44 g Romano cheese, shredded or ground

Salt

Coarsely ground black pepper

Cook the French fries as described on page 110, or use the following cheater method: Prick the potatoes with a fork and microwave them whole until cooked through, turning occasionally. Put the spuds right on the rotating platter, leaving plenty of space between them so that they will cook more evenly. If you use the baked potato setting on your microwave, remove them three-quarters of the way through the cooking time. They shouldn't be crunchy, but don't let them cross over into mushy territory or the fries will fall apart. Let cool, then cut into thumb-width sticks.

Heat ¼ inch/6 mm of canola oil in a 12-inch/30 cm skillet over medium-high heat until shimmery but not smoking. Fry the sticks, turning with tongs so that they brown evenly. When they are deliciously golden-brown (8 to 10 minutes), drain and sprinkle generously with salt and pepper.

In a salad bowl, toss the greens, onion, olive oil, a squeeze of lemon, the cheese, more salt and pepper and the fries. Turn out onto plates and enjoy your vegetables.

WEDGIE

This crispy, zippy salad is a nod to mid-'60s fine dining. Instead of iceberg lettuce, we use romaine, because it is so much tastier, and our spicy, tangy Jerry Dressing in place of your standard blue cheese, and marinate the tomato . . . as I said, it's just a nod. Still pretty great with a martini and some Mancini, though.

SERVES 2

½ head romaine lettuce

½ cup/327 ml Jerry Dressing (page 62)

¼ cup/40 g Marinated Tomato (page 217) diced

2 tbsp/17 g pickled hot banana pepper rings, drained and cut into ¼"/6 mm dice

2 tbsp/16 g red onion, sliced thinly

2 tbsp/10 g fresh parsley, chopped

Lotsa coarsely ground black pepper

2 tbsp/30 ml extra-virgin olive oil

Split the half-head of lettuce stem to tip, so you have two wedge-shaped quarters.

Place the wedges on a platter, pointy side up. Spoon the Jerry Dressing across the middle of each so that the tip and bottom stay exposed. Spoon the tomato over the base, covering the bottoms of the stems. Sprinkle the banana peppers to make a stripe across the dressing, then the onion to make another one. Sprinkle Elvis Parsley all over the plate, then the black pepper, then the oil. That's it! Eat.

Goes great with a hoppy beer, like Atlantic Brewing Co. New Guy IPA.

RENEE'S SALAD

The problem with naming any dish after someone is everybody else. "Why don't I have a dish?" they whine. Well, kids, I have no answer. Some people inspire me to invent a great dish, and some don't. This one should really be called the Fabulous Renee, because Renee Philbrook (Cafe Miranda bookkeeper and best friend) is fabulous, and so is this salad. The F.R. requested a hearty salad that was low-calorie yet satisfying. In other words, not wimpy. The result is essentially a vegan chef's salad, with lots of zingy pickled goodness. Focaccia on the side is a must!

SERVES 2

---

2 cups/60 g mixed greens

¼ cup/8 g arugula, stemmed if necessary

¼ cup/22 g radicchio, shredded

2 tbsp/18 g red onion, sliced

¼ cup/28 g hot pickled banana pepper rings

½ Roasted Red Pepper (page 221), cut into 1"/2.5 cm pieces

6 cloves garlic, roasted

¼ tsp minced fresh garlic

2 canned artichoke hearts, quartered

2 tbsp/10 g Caramelized Onions (page 220)

¼ cup/40 g Marinated Tomato (page 217)

6 fennel seeds, toasted

8 oil-cured, pitted black olives

1 generous tbsp/10 g raisins

5 tbsp/75 ml extra-virgin olive oil

¼ cup/20 g fresh parsley, chopped

2 tbsp/30 ml brine from the pepper rings

Pinch dried oregano

Toss it all together in a bowl. Let it sit to set up for a few minutes. Turn it out onto a chilled platter.

Enjoy with a tall sparkling water, as a luncheon feed that won't put you to sleep. It also makes a killer vegan wrap—just use a quarter of this recipe for each.

CHEF'S TIP: This recipe calls for some ingredients that you might not always keep on hand, like I do: a roasted pepper, caramelized onion, roasted garlic. To make them, see the Components chapter. I highly recommend cooking up big batches of each and freezing them in ice-cube trays so that you can pull them out for quick meals.

SHRIMP, AVOCADO AND THE USUAL SUSPECTS

The Usual Suspects—cabbage, lime and cilantro—is our favorite accompaniment when dishes need a little lightening and brightening. It also is a fresh-tasting, delicious salad on its own, with the addition of avocado to smooth out the flavor and texture and shrimp for protein and a briny chew. A perfect start to a summer meal or a refreshing lunch in winter, when the Maine shrimp are in season.

SERVES 4 AS AN APPETIZER, 2 AS LUNCH

1 recipe The Usual Suspects (page 101)

1 lb/454 g peeled, deveined shrimp, either Maine shrimp or 16–20 count Gulf shrimp

1 ripe avocado, pitted, peeled and diced (a little mush is OK as it distributes that delish vegetable fat)

¼ tsp cumin seeds, toasted

Bring to a boil a medium pot of salted water. Fill a similarly sized vessel with ice water. Have a strainer handy.

When the water is boiling, put in the shrimp and stir. Do not look away! I often say that cooking Maine shrimp is like riding a motorcycle. Look away and BAM—you hit a pole. Let that be a warning for both issues. While keeping your eyes on the pot, count to 40. Immediately drain the shrimp and plunge into the ice water, stirring. This is called "shocking" and immediately stops the cooking.

If you are using the 16–20 shrimp, proceed in the same way, but cook for 3 minutes. You can probably look away once or twice.

Drain the shrimp and mix with the other ingredients in a big bowl.

Pop a can of Tecate beer with salt and a lime. Enjoy that summer flavor, even while watching a three-thirty January sunset in snowy Maine.

CHEF'S TIP: Maine shrimp are sweet, tender, teeny and troublesome. In my book (and this is my book) there are only two ways to cook these critters: breaded and fried, or poached. Here, because we want a light and bright dish, we are poaching them. You can also use the more widely available Gulf shrimp (16–20 count per pound). The bigger varieties lack the sweetness of Maine shrimp but, I have to admit, are a lot easier to prepare.

SALADE CHINOISE

This is an old and simple fave, a delightful combination of flavors and textures. The broccoli brings freshness and some crunch; the Asian-style dressing is sweet and salty and spicy, and the oranges add a surprising sweet-tart pop.

SERVES 2

3 cups/240 g broccoli florets or broccolini

Olive oil

1 tsp minced fresh ginger

½ tsp minced garlic

3 tbsp/45 ml quality soy sauce

1 tbsp/15 ml mirin

⅛ tsp toasted sesame oil

15 segments of canned mandarin oranges

1 tbsp/15 ml juice from the mandarin orange can

1 scallion, cut on the bias

1 tsp sesame seeds, toasted

Roasting the broccoli gives it that lovely cooked-cabbage flavor. To roast: Preheat your oven to 425°F/218°C. Toss the broccoli in olive oil to coat. Roast on a cookie sheet until tender, 10 to 15 minutes. You want bright color, so don't overcook it. You don't want that olive drab.

While the broccoli is cooking, mix all the other ingredients in a bowl. When the broccoli is done, add it to the bowl. Toss everything together and turn out on a platter. Serve warm, at room temperature, or cold.

CHEF'S TIP: You can also steam the broccoli instead of roasting to make it more genteel. Just place it in a steamer over boiling water and steam until tender, about 5 minutes.

CHOWDER GUY

The word *guy* is used in a particular way on the coast of Maine. It's perhaps closest to *man* or *dude* elsewhere. So, if someone asks, "What the heck is that?" I could answer "Chowder guy," and thus imply that it should be obvious. This doesn't look like your traditional chowder; it's better, and easier. Instead of small pieces of seafood and potato swimming in milky broth, this reduces the broth to a creamy sauce and pours it over whole clams, potatoes and corn.

SERVES 2

3 oz/85 g uncooked quality thick-cut bacon, chopped coarsely

½ cup/66 g onion, sliced

1 clove garlic, minced

3 tbsp/45 ml olive oil

3 medium red potatoes, boiled (OK, microwave them!), cooled and cubed

8 littleneck clams, well washed

1 cup plus 2 tbsp/265 ml fish stock or low-sodium clam juice

½ cup plus 2 tbsp/150 ml heavy cream

¼ cup/37 g fresh corn kernels, cut from the cob (frozen will do)

2 sprigs thyme

Salt

Coarsely ground black pepper

2 drizzles (½ tsp each) aged balsamic vinegar

2 tbsp/30 ml extra-virgin olive oil

Crusty bread, to serve

Preheat your oven to 375°F/191°C. In a heavy oven-safe casserole dish at least 12 inches/30 cm in diameter, place the bacon, onion, garlic and olive oil. Pop it in the oven.

Go open a craft brew, sip. Yes, this is a "roasted" chowder. That means you have time to kick back while it cooks.

When the dish has heated up and the onion, etc., has begun to fry (about 10 minutes), add the potatoes, coating them with the olive oil and the now-rendering bacon. Smells good, eh?

Sip more beer.

Keep an eye on the casserole as the onion sweats (meaning it's not browning, though browned would be good, too). After about 10 minutes, when the onion is translucent (tan at most), put the beer down and add your starring seafood. Add the stock, cream, corn and thyme. Put it back in the oven. Cook until the liquid is close to boiling and the clams are open, about 15 minutes. Salt and pepper to taste (you shouldn't need much salt, as a lot will come from the bacon).

Spoon into heated soup bowls. Drizzle with the balsamic and extra-virgin olive oil. Serve with a crusty bread and yet more beer.

CHEF'S TIP: This recipe works with all kinds of seafood. Try substituting a dozen mussels or 8 ounces/225 g of fish (we use haddock; you can try salmon, if you want to go New Age). If you have lobster stock on hand, by all means substitute it for the fish stock.

WHITE BEAN SOUP

Here is another of our instant soups, ready to be made up on demand. I think this one is just the epitome of what soup should be. It's brothy but substantial from the beans, with the healthy chew of kale and a little zing of fresh tomato to balance it out. It really takes the edge off a Maine winter evening.

SERVES 1

1 cup/180 g kale, stemmed and ripped into bite-size pieces

Olive oil

¾ cup/170 g White Bean Ragout (page 213)

2 tbsp/20 g Marinated Tomato (page 217) or chopped fresh tomato

1½ cups/355 ml vegetable or chicken stock

Sprig of fresh herb (try thyme, rosemary or tarragon)

Focaccia (page 159), to serve

Toss the kale with a drizzle of olive oil and leave to sit. This is best done ahead of time, as the oil will tenderize the kale. You can keep oiled kale in your fridge for several days and pull out a handful when you need it.

Preheat your oven to 375°F/191°C. In a 7-inch/18 cm oven-safe casserole dish, combine the ragout, tomato and stock. Put the kale on top. Put the dish in the oven so the soup heats while the kale roasts. When the kale has darkened and shriveled and gotten a bit crispy at the edges, 5 to 8 minutes, your soup is done.

Tip it out into a warm bowl. Give it a good healthy squirt of decent olive oil and float the herb sprig on top. Serve with a Pellegrino and a chunk of focaccia.

LENTIL SOUP

This soup is exotic yet comfortable. It's great for cold days, of course, but also for hot ones: It will make you sweat and cool you off, by the principle of evaporative cooling. It is based off our Lentil Doll, which is a version of the spiced lentil slurry that goes by the name of dal on the subcontinent. Once you have the Doll made, this soup is practically instant.

SERVES 2 AS A MEAL, 4 AS A STARTER

2 cups/473 ml Lentil Doll (page 214)

2 cups/473 ml chicken or vegetable stock

¼ cup/40 g Marinated Tomato (page 217) or chopped fresh tomato

2 cups/60 g spinach, stemmed and tossed in olive oil

¼ cup/60 ml plain yogurt

¼ cup/56 g seeded or Euro cucumber, shredded

4 sprigs cilantro

1 tsp sesame seeds, toasted

Lemon wedges

Extra-virgin olive oil

Place a medium saucepan over medium heat. Place the Doll, stock and tomato in the pan; bring to a boil. Add the spinach and stir to wilt, just for a minute. Dish out into warm bowls. Distribute the yogurt into each. Add a pile of cukes on top of the yogurt, then the cilantro, then sprinkle the seeds. Serve with lemon on the side.

Accompany this with a strong tea and it can take you out of a 10°F/–12°C day to warm, exotic places. This vacation courtesy of food.

NO EXCUSES

This is another one of our "stealth vegetarian" dishes. As a matter of fact, it's vegan and gluten-free. You won't miss a thing. No excuses! It's a rich coconut-curry broth, packed with fresh vegetables and rice noodles. It's colorful, aromatic, flavorful, hot and comforting; fine eating for a winter night. The most time here goes to prepping the vegetables. After that, the cooking is practically instant.

SERVES 2

2½ cups/591 ml coconut milk

2 to 3 tbsp/29 to 44 g panang curry paste (get Maesri brand, if possible)

¼ cup/30 g carrot, cut into 4"/10 cm matchsticks

3 cups/710 ml vegetable stock

⅛ cup/20 g red sweet pepper, seeded and ripped into bite-size chunks

8 largish button mushrooms, quartered

6 oz/170 g firm tofu, cut into 1" x 4"/ 1.3 x 10 cm sticks

1 tsp fresh ginger, minced

1 tsp garlic, minced

3 cups/100 g loosely packed lacinato kale, stemmed and ripped up

8 leaves Thai basil (or whatever basil you have)

1 cup/100 g fresh wide rice noodles, cut into 1½"/4 cm strips (it's OK to be a bit irregular)

2 tsp/10 ml vegetarian Thai fish sauce

4 sprigs cilantro

¼ cup/26 g mung bean sprouts

1 tsp black sesame seeds

¼ lime, or more to taste

Place a heavy-bottomed nonreactive pan over medium-high heat. I use a 6-quart/ 6 L Dutch oven for this. Put in ¾ cup/177 ml of the coconut milk. You are going to render the fat from the coconut milk to use as a frying medium. As it heats, the watery part of the milk will evaporate, leaving the fat behind. You'll see it start to boil, and then stop when the water is gone. This will take 8 to 10 minutes.

In go the curry paste and carrot. Fry, but do not brown. It will smell magnificent! This should go on for about 2 minutes.

Add the stock and the remaining coconut milk. Bring to a boil. Then add the red pepper, mushrooms and tofu. Simmer until they are hot throughout, 3 minutes or so. Add the ginger, garlic, kale, basil and noodles. Stir gently as needed while you heat the mixture for 4 minutes or so.

Ladle into high-sided Asian-style bowls. Drizzle in some fish sauce; top with the cilantro, bean sprouts and sesame seeds; and squeeze the lime over. Serve the food with Asian style spoons and chopsticks.

Maine Root Ginger Brew makes for a perfect combo.

CHEF'S TIP: Thai fish sauce is available in vegetarian versions (like jumbo shrimp, it's an oxymoron, but you do what you have to). Both kinds are available in Asian groceries, as are the fresh rice noodles, usually sold as a sheet.

ROASTED BROCCOLI, CORN AND BLUE CHEESE SOUP

The words *broccoli* and *cheese* together in the name of a soup conjure visions of a thick cafeteria cup of mud that you can stand a spoon in. This isn't that. It's brothy, creamy, with a hint of blue-cheese funk, a hit of fried onions and real florets of broccoli. In fact, this is a multiutensil soup, best served with a spoon, fork and knife to manage the vegetables. We make this with the broccoli we grow on Headacre Farm and corn from Weskeag Farm down the road. Super-fresh vegetables will give you a stupendous soup, but this preparation also makes the most of the produce your grocery store carries in the middle of winter.

SERVES 2

1½ cups/106 g broccoli florets, cut to the size of golf balls

¼ cup/33 g red onion, sliced

Olive oil

⅓ cup/54 g fresh corn kernels, cut from the cob

1 tsp garlic, minced

1 cup/236 ml heavy cream

1 cup/236 ml chicken stock

2 tbsp/30 ml white wine

2 leaves basil

1½ oz/43 g blue cheese crumbles (the cheap ones)

Preheat your oven to 400°F/204°C.

In a 7- to 9-inch/18 to 23 cm oven-safe casserole dish, toss the broccoli and onion in olive oil to coat. Put in the oven and roast, stirring occasionally, for about 8 minutes, until the onion is light brown and the broccoli is changing to a really dark green. Stir in the corn and garlic. Remove the dish from the oven and let it calm down for a few minutes.

Add the cream, stock, wine, basil and blue cheese and return to the oven for 2 minutes, to heat through. Check to make sure the broccoli is fork-tender; if not, cook longer.

Plate in heated bowls and drizzle olive oil over the top. Serve with a sharp, refreshing mineral water.

THE LATEST (VEGAN EDITION)

This dish embodies the briny goodness and invigorating flavors of the cold, clear waters of Maine. It's a gingery miso broth filled with soba noodles, tofu, beech mushrooms and sweet kelp. We get the seaweed locally, of course! See the following recipe for an equally delicious but heartier version made with shellfish and pork.

SERVES 2

1½ oz/43 g soba noodles

1 oz/28 g beech, oyster or shiitake mushrooms

4 oz/113 g firm tofu

3 oz/85 g fresh or frozen sweet sea kelp

2 cups/473 ml water

2 tbsp/30 ml mirin

½ tsp fresh ginger, minced

½ tsp garlic, minced

1½ tbsp/26 g miso

¼ cup/26 g mung bean sprouts

½ lemon

1 scallion, sliced on the bias

½ tsp sesame oil

Boil the soba noodles in salted water according to the package directions. Drain and reserve.

Beech or oyster mushrooms can be left whole. If you are using shiitake mushrooms, slice them up, no stems. Cut the tofu and kelp into bite-size pieces.

In a shallow 4-quart/4 L saucepan, place the 2 cups/473 ml of water and the mirin, ginger and garlic. Cover and bring to a boil. Once boiling, add the tofu and mushrooms. Remove from the heat. Stir in the miso. Add the kelp and reserved soba, then cover and let rest for 5 minutes. There is enough heat in the broth to cook the soup; miso should never be boiled.

Place the sprouts in 2 large flat-bottomed bowls. Pour half of the contents of the pan into each. Garnish them with squeezes of lemon, the sliced scallion and a drizzle of sesame oil. Serve with large spoons and chopsticks.

THE LATEST (WITH PORK AND SHELLFISH)

Here is the bulked-up version of The Latest. Slim strips of pork loin, whitefish, shrimp and mussels make it a real feast suspended in the same light, flavorful miso broth. This makes a lovely meal for two or a starter for four.

SERVES 2 TO 4

1½ oz/43 g soba noodles

2 cups/473 ml water or seafood stock

1 oz/28 g beech, oyster or shiitake mushrooms

3 oz/85 g fresh or frozen sweet sea kelp

2 tbsp/30 ml mirin

½ tsp fresh ginger, minced

½ tsp garlic, minced

4 oz/113 g peeled and deveined shrimp

4 oz/113 g white fish, such as hake, cusk, haddock or cod, cut into bite-size pieces

18 mussels, cleaned and debearded

2 oz/67 g pork loin, cut into ¼"/6 mm strips

1½ tbsp/26 g miso

¼ cup/26 g mung bean sprouts

½ lemon

1 scallion, sliced on the bias

½ tsp sesame oil

Boil the soba noodles in salted water according to the package directions. Drain and reserve.

Beech or oyster mushrooms can be left whole. If you are using shiitake mushrooms, slice them up. Cut the kelp into chopstickable pieces.

In a shallow 4-quart/4-liter saucepan, place the 2 cups/473 ml of water and the mirin, ginger and garlic. Cover and bring to a boil. Once boiling, add the shrimp, fish and mussels. Lower the heat to a simmer and cook for 6 to 8 minutes, until the mussels are just opening. The shrimp should be half-done. Add the pork and mushrooms, then remove from the heat. Stir in the miso. Add kelp and soba, then cover and let rest for several minutes. The pork will cook in the residual heat; if you try to boil it, it will get tough. Plus, miso should never be boiled.

Place the sprouts in large flat-bottomed bowls. Pour the contents of the pan into each. Garnish them with a squeeze of lemon, the sliced scallion and a drizzle of sesame oil. Serve with large spoons and chopsticks.

MIRANDA'S "RANCH" DRESSING

Do you like ranch dressing? If not, try this recipe. It's much more interesting than your typical crudité dip: tangy from lemon, spicy from pepper relish, flavored with onion, garlic and dill. I invented it to serve with fried food and called it ranch so people would feel comfortable with it. I'd say, "Sorry for the bait and switch," but I'm not. What's a little deception, when it gives you a dressing this good?

MAKES 1⅔ QUARTS/1.5L

1 (30 oz/950 ml) jar mayonnaise (a cheap brand is OK; use Kewpie if you have the supply and the dough)

8 oz/227 g hot pepper relish (such as Cento brand)

2 tsp/5 g paprika

2 tsp/2 g dried dill

¼ cup/28 g dried onion

¼ cup/55 ml freshly squeezed lemon juice

2 tsp/6 g garlic powder

Mix all the ingredients together. An electric hand or stand mixer fitted with a whisk works well.

Use this sauce on a Reuben, for dipping fries or onion rings, to accompany fish or crab cakes or just to dress a salad.

CHEF'S TIP: This makes a big batch of dressing for you to keep in the fridge. For a single-dish version with a slightly different flavor profile, see the 50 MPH Tomatoes (page 18).

JERRY DRESSING

This is our variation on blue cheese dressing. Hot and red peppers give it heat and sweetness, as well as an appealingly chunky texture. There's also an intriguing herbal element contributed by fresh basil. Use it wherever you'd use blue cheese dressing: as a dip, with hot wings or on a crunchy salad. Try it on a burger, too!

MAKES 1⅔ QUARTS/1.5L

4 whole cloves garlic

3 tbsp/45 ml juice from jar of hot pickled banana peppers

5 leaves basil

2½ oz/71 g blue cheese (use the cheap stuff)

5 tbsp/72 g sour cream

¼ cup/99 g hot pickled banana pepper rings, drained and chopped

½ roasted red pepper, diced (canned if ya gotta)

1 tsp coarsely ground black pepper

Place the garlic, pepper juice and basil in a blender. Puree. Transfer to a medium bowl and add the blue cheese. Beat with a whisk to break up the cheese and then whisk in the sour cream. Add all the kinds of pepper.

This dressing can be refrigerated for several days.

3

PASTA

I grew up in an Italian-American community, and so did my love of food. Nothing says *comfort* to me like a plate of fresh pasta with big, tender meatballs (Spaghetti Wit, as I call it). This chapter presents some of the recipes of my past—my Nanna Connie's meatballs, Auntie Fluffie's Pasta—and a lot more that have evolved in the decades I've been cooking. Pasta is a perfect canvas for local and seasonal ingredients, so you'll find a recipe for the brief fiddlehead season and Jalunkies, based on wild mushrooms, as well as Simply Delish, which features our local crab, and, of course, Lobster Mac 'n Cheese. But I cook year-round, including the times when nothing grows here, so there are anytime recipes, too: Lamb and Lentil, the ultra-rich Old Bleu and a classic Bolognese. Many (but not all) are best with homemade pasta, so why not start there?

Please don't shy away if boxed pasta is all that's available; just substitute 3 ounces/85 g of dried pasta for 4 ounces/113 g of fresh.

FRESH PASTA

Fresh pasta is really something special. There's nothing wrong with a box of spaghetti, but these soft, eggy, chewy noodles are something else entirely. The porousness of the noodles allows them to absorb and bind with sauces in a way dried noodles can't. The process requires a pasta machine and a bit of time, but it is worth every penny and every moment.

The ratio of eggs to flour is critical in this recipe. For pasta, we measure the eggs by weight, which I know is an unusual thing to do, but it is that important. For the same reason I recommend measuring the flour by weight. A cup of flour can vary by up to an ounce/28 g, and that can make or break a recipe. If you don't have a kitchen scale, you can measure the eggs by volume instead. Then go buy a kitchen scale for the flour.

This recipe makes enough pasta for two to three servings. If you need more, make it in separate batches. It's a very stiff dough and a big batch will overload the mixer. I do recommend making as much as you can. You can refrigerate the fresh pasta for up to a week, or freeze it for much longer.

MAKES 12 OZ/340 G PASTA

3¾ cup/652 g semolina flour
5 tsp/21 g sea salt
1¼ cups/293 ml eggs, lightly beaten (about 5 large eggs)

In the bowl of a standing mixer fitted with the dough hook, place the flour, salt and most of the eggs, reserving about 2 tablespoons/29 ml, or about half an egg. Mix on slow speed until the dough comes together in a tight ball. If it becomes grainy and looks like coarse meal, add the reserved egg and continue to mix. If it still doesn't work, crack another egg, beat it and add teaspoons at a time until the dough comes together. When it forms a ball, it's done.

Remove the dough from the mixer and form it into a small loaf. Wrap it in plastic, and refrigerate overnight (or up to a week). This will let the flour hydrate and stabilize. If necessary, you can skip the chilling, but the results won't be quite as good.

When you are ready to roll the pasta, take the loaf from the refrigerator and use a sharp knife to cut it into ¼-inch/6 mm slices. Run each slice through your pasta machine, gradually decreasing the thickness until between ⅛ inch/3 mm and 1/16 inch/1.5 mm. For linguine or other noodles, use the crank to cut the pasta to the desired width. For papardelle, use a knife to cut the rolled sheets of pasta into random large noodles. Attacking the sheet with a pizza cutter is also quite fun, if you're into that sort of thing.

At this point, you can refrigerate the pasta for a number of days, or it can go right into a large pot of boiling salted water. Cook for 3 to 5 minutes, or until al dente. If you want to keep the pasta longer, divide it into portions, wrap and freeze. Cook it straight out of the freezer, without thawing. The cooking time will be close to the same.

The very best way to eat this pasta, in my opinion, is hot out of pot, with salt and a little butter. If you don't eat the whole batch that way, try some of the sauces in this chapter.

AGGABLAGGA

This recipe was inspired by Primo, Rockland's wonderful farm-to-table fine dining establishment. Melissa Kelly (who wrote our foreword) was serving pasta with a simple tomato sauce and crispy calamari. It killed me. I went home and reconstructed it for my restaurant. When it came time to put it on the menu, I couldn't call it "stolen from Primo," so I took the advice of my then-toddler son and went with Aggablagga.

This is the epitome of the rustic Mediterranean style that Melissa has turned into an art form. It is full of fresh flavors and textures, healthy, quick and inexpensive (especially if you use frozen squid, often available at Asian markets). I've done it for weeknight family meals and for dinner parties. Aggablagga always wins.

SERVES 2

10 oz/283 g Fresh Pasta (page 64)

8 oz/227 g squid, cleaned and drained

2 cups/350 g semolina flour

Olive oil, for frying

2 tsp/10 g red pepper flakes

Handful of spinach (about 1.5 cups/50 g)

1 tbsp/30 ml extra-virgin olive oil

1 cup/237 ml Latex Marinara (page 218), warmed

1 tbsp/9 g garlic, minced

2 sprigs oregano, or a tiny pinch dried

Lemon wedges

Bring a pot of water to a boil, salt and add the pasta. Cook to al dente according to the pasta recipe or package directions, then drain and return to the pot.

Slice the squid into bite-size rings and pieces. Toss it with the semolina to coat.

Heat ¼ inch/6 mm of olive oil in a large skillet over medium-high heat. It needs to be over 300°F/149°C, but shouldn't smoke. Add the squid. Don't touch it too much. Leave it alone for a minute, then flip it once. When golden, toss in the garlic and oregano, lightly browning the garlic. Transfer to a heated plate (not paper towels). Some of the coating will fall off—just a nice delicate one will remain.

To the noodles in the pot, add the red pepper flakes, spinach and the good olive oil. Toss well and let the spinach wilt.

Spread the marinara sauce on a platter. Top with the pasta mixture, then the calamari. Serve with lemon wedges. Sinatra will be singing in your head.

NEIL ANDERSON'S BOLOGNESE OF AUGUST

Neil Anderson was the second chef I ever hired. He came into the restaurant one day, turned to the waitress and said, "I want to work here." We took him on. During Neil's first summer, I told him we were going to make Bolognese sauce. "Right," said Neil. "We are making Bolognese, and you are going to go sweat over it." He was not incorrect that heavy, long-cooked meat sauces are not entirely appropriate for the dog days, but I am contrary. Neil is now a professor of languages somewhere, and every summer we make this out of season in his honor.

This is our version of a traditional Bolognese: a meat sauce flavored with a bit of tomato. It is not the red sauce with meat that sometimes gets called by the same name. Through long cooking, the meats gain a velvety texture and a flavor so addictive that you won't be able to stop eating it, no matter what the weather.

SERVES 3 TO 4

½ cup/120 ml olive oil

4 cloves garlic

⅛ tsp fennel seeds

½ onion, sliced

1 rib celery, chopped coarsely

½ cup/60 g carrot, cut into medium dice

4 oz/113 g ground veal

4 oz/113 g ground pork

1 (28 oz/794 g) can tomatoes

2 tbsp/33 g tomato paste

½ cup/118 ml heavy cream

1 lb/454 g dried rigatoni pasta, cooked

Place a 4-quart/4 L nonreactive pot over medium-high heat. Heat the olive oil and add the garlic; fry until the cloves are almost golden, 4 minutes. Add the fennel seeds, count to 3, and drop in the onion, celery and carrot. Sweat the vegetables in the olive oil until they are sweet and the garlic is soft, about 10 minutes. Add the veal and pork, breaking up with a spoon to distribute the meat and vegetables as evenly as you can (you'll mash it later).

When the meat is cooked (it should take 10 to 12 minutes) add the tomatoes, tomato paste and ½ cup/118 ml of water. Turn down the heat to low and simmer for at least an hour, preferably 2. Mash with a potato masher to break everything up until it looks like a sauce.

Add the cream. If you'll be storing the sauce, wait to add the cream until reheating.

For this dish, I prefer boxed rigatoni (not homemade noodles). Add the cooked noodles to the pot of sauce and stir carefully so that you don't break any noodles. Distribute onto plates, pour some red wine and eat.

CHEF'S TIP: For foolproof seasoning: Remove a small amount of the sauce and add some salt and pepper until it tastes perfect. Using this as a guide, add salt and pepper by small amounts to the pot until it matches the sample.

CLASSIC GOODNESS

The name says it all. This recipe came from one of our former chefs, David Joseph, who now sells the best handmade donuts in Maine at Rockland's Willow Bake Shoppe. This man knows classic goodness when he sees it.

The dish is pasta, garlic and olive oil. You OK with dat? Oh, greens, too. The dish is perfect just like that, or you can add mussels or shrimp to make it extra special.

SERVES 1

6 oz/171 g fresh linguine

Olive oil

2 anchovies

2 tbsp/18 g garlic, minced

¼ lb/113 g mussels, cleaned and debearded, or 6 oz/170 g cleaned shrimp (optional)

¼ cup/60 ml dry white wine

2 cups/60 g spinach, stemmed

Salt

Coarsely ground black pepper

2 oz/57 g ricotta salata, shaved

Cook the pasta in boiling salted water until al dente. Drain and toss with olive oil.

Coat a 12-inch/30 cm sauté pan with ⅛ inch/3 mm of olive oil. Place over medium heat.

This one is fast, so pay attention! When the oil is hot, in go the anchovies. Stir to break them apart. They will sizzle and then the sizzle will start to lessen as the water evaporates, 1 to 2 minutes.

Add the garlic, stirring always. Let it brown to a mahogany color, about a minute.

If you aren't using mussels or shrimp, proceed past the next two lines.

Shrimp option: Add the shrimp to the pan and sauté for about 4 minutes, until opaque.

Mussel option: Put the mussels in the pan and stir to coat (splatter alert), then cover and shake the pan. They are done when they open, after about 5 minutes.

Remove from the heat. Add the wine and stir to stop the cooking process (another splatter alert!). Add the spinach and return to the heat. Stir for a minute or two to wilt the spinach. Add the cooked pasta and toss well. Season with salt and pepper.

Plate on a warm platter. Sprinkle with the cheese, unless you have included the fish. *Non formaggi con pesce!* In either case, drizzle with olive oil.

Chilled Pinot Grigio and yummmmmmmmm.

AUNTIE FLUFFIE'S PASTA

My Auntie Fluffie (that is, Ms. Florence Altiero-Madafarri) lives in Hollywood, Florida, with her ceramic leopards and leopard-print plates. But back in the '60s she was a classic babe-in-miniskirt, with a Princess phone and spit curls. In that era, Fluff lived next door to my family, and she would feed my brother and me food like this recipe. This is a "cream of leftovers" dish that you can throw together on a weeknight. Still, it's memorable. It's got all the good stuff: browned butter, caramelized onion, lemon and cheese; cauliflower is the star. If you think you don't like cauliflower, I dare you to give it a try.

SERVES 2

½ cup/112 g (1 stick) butter (yup)

½ red onion, diced

2 tsp garlic, minced

1½ cups/350 g cauliflower, cut into forkfuls

½ lb/225 g pasta, preferably rigatoni, cooked

½ cup/40 g fresh parsley, chopped coarsely

½ lemon

Salt

Coarsely ground black pepper

Romano or Parmesan cheese, grated

Place a heavy 12-inch/30 cm skillet over medium-high heat. Put in the butter, onion, garlic and cauliflower. Partially cover the pan and simultaneously brown the butter, caramelize the onion and get the cauliflower cooked. It will take around 10 minutes. They are all kind of racing each other. If the onion is browning but the cauliflower isn't tender, add a splash of white wine or water and cover until the cauliflower is steamed through.

Add the pasta and stir; heat through. Add the parsley, squeeze in the lemon and stir. Turn out the pasta onto a warm platter. Sprinkle with salt, pepper and cheese.

DON'T EAT ME AGAIN, JOEL!

Joel Hokkanen and his wife, Rebecca, may be the handsomest and most rascalish couple I know. They have been customers since even before we opened. They are in the legal business and helped us close on our building on Oak Street, along with all those other law issues that came up around the restaurant's opening.

This dish was on our first menu, where it was called "Smoked Turkey w/Caramelized Onion, Browned Mushrooms, Basil, Marsala, Mascarpone Cream and Our Fresh Pasta." It is creamy, rich and comforting, with the sweetness of caramelized onions contrasting with the smoky turkey. Joel and Rebecca were always sophisticated eaters (especially for 1990s midcoast Maine), and they are always cruising the menu for new and interesting dishes. Well, Rebecca is. Joel stopped with this one. We named the dish for him when it became clear that he would never order anything different.

SERVES 2

10 oz/283 g Fresh Pasta (page 64)

9 medium white mushrooms

6 tbsp/90 ml olive oil

¾ cup/99 g red onion, sliced

3 cloves garlic, minced

6 oz/170 g smoked turkey, diced or shredded

¼ cup/60 ml marsala wine

½ cup/120 g mascarpone cheese

4 leaves basil

Salt

Coarsely ground black pepper

Cook the pasta to al dente according to the pasta recipe directions. Drain, reserving a half-cup of the cooking water. Do not rinse.

Smash the mushrooms: Put them on the counter and use your clenched fist to bop them and break them into random pieces. Great fun for kids!

Heat the olive oil in a 12-inch/30 cm skillet over medium-high heat. Add the onion and cook until almost as soft and translucent as you want it, 4 to 5 minutes. Then introduce the garlic, sauté for another minute and add the mushrooms. Let the mushrooms cook about halfway, that is to say, just browning a little, with the texture relaxing. This will take about 3 minutes. Add the turkey.

Now we leave this alone, in the pan, on the heat. The idea is to brown the heck out of the whole mixture. Brown, brown, brown. Resist the urge to mess with this. Certainly observe to make sure it doesn't scorch, but the product needs time and surfaces touching the heat so they can reach 300°F/149°C to caramelize. If you see it starting to burn, you can stir. Be prepared for spattering.

When it is good and brown, not quiiiite burnt, remove from the heat. This will take 7 or 8 minutes. Let it calm down a little bit. Stir in the marsala and mascarpone. This mixture will, as our former cook Neal Anderson would exclaim, "Bind the fat with fat!" Yum. Return to the heat. If the sauce breaks—that is, separates—add a bit of the pasta water. This will rebind it.

Toss in the basil leaves. Add the pasta and toss well. Plate on a warmed plate. Sprinkle with salt and pepper.

BTP (BACON/ TOMATO/PEAS)

Here we have a pasta dish made of the simplest, most familiar ingredients that come together into something entirely irresistible. What is better than bacon, peas and tomato tossed wit fresh pasta? Yes—bacon, peas and tomato in a cream sauce tossed with fresh pasta!

You can use frozen peas for this, but when we have fresh ones from Headacre Farm, they make a big difference.

SERVES 2

Olive oil

5 oz/142 g uncooked quality bacon, cut into ½"/1.5 cm chunks

½ cup/66 g red onion, sliced

1 oz/28 g garlic, minced (4 to 5 cloves)

½ cup/80 g Marinated Tomato (page 217)

⅓ cup/78 ml heavy cream

12 oz/340 g Fresh Pasta (page 64), formed into linguine

½ cup/67 g fresh or frozen peas

8 leaves basil

¼ cup/44 g Romano cheese, grated

Heat a large pot of water for the pasta.

Coat the bottom of a 12-inch/30 cm skillet with olive oil and place over medium-high heat. Add the bacon and sauté to brown it, stirring occasionally, about 5 minutes. Add the onion and brown it, too (8 minutes). Add the garlic and stir for just a minute, until golden. Add the tomato and stir. Cook for 2 more minutes.

Add the cream and continue cooking for 5 minutes or so, until it reduces to a sauce that will coat a spoon. Turn off the heat and park it.

Cook the pasta to al dente according to the pasta recipe directions. Drain.

Reheat the sauce if it has cooled down. Add the peas and basil. Toss with the cooked pasta. Dump the lot onto a warm platter and sprinkle Romano all around.

Burp!

LOBSTER MAC 'N CHEESE

This dish is not your usual brick of noodles and cheese sauce. It's a casserole made with fresh pasta and a creamy sauce, with some greens and tomato to add a bit of an edge. It's simple: You just put all the ingredients in a pan and put it in the oven until all that good cheese, cream and noodle bubble together into a fabulously rich, tender, comforting dish. Adding lobster pushes it right over the top.

You have to have this right out of the oven. You can reheat it and it will still be a great mac 'n cheese, but out of the oven it is just transcendent. If you are reheating, adding a touch of water will help it all come back together.

SERVES 1 TO 2

4½ oz/128 g Fresh Pasta (page 64), cooked slightly past al dente

3 oz/85 g mozzarella cheese, shredded

1 oz/28 g Romano or Parmesan cheese, shredded or grated

¼ cup/40 g fresh tomato, diced

3½ oz/104 ml heavy cream

Salt

Coarsely ground black pepper

Dash marsala, port or sherry

1 leaf basil

1½ cups/45 g loosely packed hearty greens, torn to bite-size, and tossed in olive oil (spinach and kale are good here)

3 oz/85 g cooked lobster meat

Preheat your oven to 350°F/177°C.

In a 9-inch/23 cm oven-safe casserole dish, mix everything together but the greens and lobster. Bake until the sauce has become thick, 8 minutes, then sprinkle the greens over the top. Continue to bake until golden brown, another 8 minutes. By the time it is browned well, the cheese and cream will have interacted with the starch in the pasta and made a sauce that will coat a spoon.

When the dish is turning brown, poke the lobster pieces into the top. Just cook it for a couple of minutes after this—you don't want the lobster to turn into little erasers.

Want to go even farther over the top? Add some raw bacon to the top of the casserole before it goes into the oven and cook it all together.

NEXT DAY AIR

I was reminded of this dish recently when I ran into a Cafe Miranda alum at Rock City Coffee, our preferred supplier since dinosaurs roamed the earth. Nate, now in his 30s, worked with us as a rebellious teen. He is one of many who have been through the CM Total Perspective Vortex and came out better for it (as am I). This is an example of how we think: simple ingredients (some of which are on hand in the freezer), combined into something that is more than the sum of its parts . . . and a juvenile joke to cap it all off. Back in the day, it took Nate awhile to get the joke.

If you substitute dried pasta, this makes a great vegan dish.

SERVES 2

10 oz/283 g Fresh Pasta (page 64), formed into pappardelle and cut into random, squarish shapes of around 2"/5 cm

Olive oil

2 cups/264 g onion, sliced

2 cups/178 g cabbage, cut like the pasta

1 tbsp/9 g garlic, minced

1 cup/237 ml White Bean Ragout (page 213)

½ cup/40 g fresh parsley, chopped coarsely (check out the tip below)

Salt

Boil salted water for the pasta. Drop in the pappardelle. Cook to al dente, drain and toss in a little olive oil to coat the noodles. Set aside.

Heat your trusty 12-inch/30 cm skillet over medium-high heat. Put in enough olive oil to coat the pan to an ⅛-inch/3 mm depth. Add the onion. Cook until just past clear but just short of browning, about 7 minutes. Add the cabbage. Stir. Then, patience. Stir occasionally until the cabbage is nice and brown, another 7 minutes.

Clear a space in the pan. Put in the garlic and a little olive oil, and stir briefly to sauté. Just as it begins to brown, stir into the greater cabbageness. Check to see whether the cabbage is cooked through. You want both it and the onion to be browned and sweet. If there's still some crunch, put a cover on the pan and continue to cook, stirring occasionally, until it is all soft and delicious.

Heat the ragout in whatever way is convenient. I use the microwave in summer and the woodstove in winter. Spread on a heated platter.

Stir the parsley into the cabbage, toss with the pasta, then pile the mixture in the center of the plate. Drizzle olive oil over all.

CHEF'S TIP: By now you know the parsley should always be cut coarsely. I despise the "green dirt" parsley minced so it has no texture and the flavor is literally washed out. Enough ranting . . . don't get me started on the New Parsley, microgreens.

FIDDLEHEAD PASTA

This is a simple sauté that is very seasonal and way yummy. Foraged food is rare in our modern world, but here in Maine we get to cook with mushrooms, fiddleheads, ramps, mussels and so on. Fiddleheads, the sprouts of certain ferns, are available for a very short time in the spring (unless you think ahead and freeze them). If you can't find them, substitute asparagus for a different but still delicious pasta.

SERVES 1

5 oz/142 g Fresh Pasta (page 64) (dried works in a pinch)

6 to 8 tbsp/90 to 120 ml extra-virgin olive oil

½ red sweet pepper, seeded and ripped coarsely

¼ red onion, sliced

1 cup/227 g fiddleheads, picked over and washed

1 to 2 cloves garlic, minced

Coarse salt

Coarsely ground black pepper

1 lemon wedge

2 oz/57 g ricotta salata, shaved

Cook the pasta in boiling salted water until al dente. Drain. Hold it while you sauté the other stuff. If you are using dried pasta, start it early, because it will take longer to cook than the sauté does.

Heat a 12-inch/30 cm sauté pan on medium to high heat. Put in 3 tablespoons/45 ml of olive oil, to coat the bottom of the pan well. Toss in the red pepper and sauté for about 3 minutes, stirring occasionally, until the color brightens. Add the onion and sauté until it sweats—that is, starts getting clear and releasing that great cooked-onion smell, another 3 minutes. Add the fiddleheads and garlic and continue to sauté for 3 minutes more. You will see the color in the fiddleheads intensify and get bright green.

Turn off the heat, add the pasta, toss well and plate on a heated plate. Dress with more olive oil, liberal amounts of the salt and black pepper and a squeeze of lemon. Top with the cheese.

CHEF'S TIP: If you would like to add some animal protein, Maine crabmeat is a charm with this one. Chicken breast works, too.

JALUNKIES

Being partly of Eastern European extraction meant I grew up in a culture (?!) that loved to forage for "jalunkies"—wild mushrooms. When we started getting foraged mushrooms from a pal in the late '90s, the common response was, "Eeeeew, weird!" We could not sell them or give them away. Now we put them on the menu under names like "chanterelle" and "hen of the woods," along with the word "foraged" and have a guaranteed sell-out.

For this preparation, use a firmer mushroom variety, such as matsutake, hen of the woods or lobster mushroom. These hold their shape better than, for example, chanterelles or black trumpets. That means they can be introduced early in the process and fully flavor the dish.

SERVES 2

½ lb/227 g dried penne or rigatoni pasta

⅔ cup/150 ml olive oil, plus more to finish

½ lb/227 g firm wild mushrooms, cleaned and cut into ½"/1.5 cm pieces

1 oz/28 g garlic, minced (about 5 cloves)

1 tsp red pepper flakes

1 cup/30 g arugula, stemmed if necessary

Sea salt

6 tbsp/89 ml Latex Marinara (page 218)

Cook the pasta in boiling salted water according to the package directions and drain.

Meanwhile, heat a 12-inch/30 cm sauté pan on medium-high heat. Pour in the ⅔ cup/150 ml of oil, then add the mushrooms. Sauté until tender, 5 minutes or so.

Push the mushrooms to the side of the pan so the bottom is clear, and tip the pan so the oil forms a puddle near the handle. Add the garlic to the puddle. Now pay attention! You want to stir as needed to evenly toast the garlic in the olive oil until it is golden brown. Remove from the heat.

Add the pasta, red pepper flakes and arugula; salt and toss. Put it back on the heat and add the marinara; toss again.

Plate on a nice warm platter or flat-bottomed pasta-serving bowl.

Good bread, a cool Pellegrino, *mangia*.

LAMB AND LENTIL PASTA

This is an unusual pasta sauce, but it is comforting and, surprisingly, quite light. The sauce is made of Lentil Doll spruced up with ground lamb, tomatoes and a whole lot of parsley. It has a lovely Mediterranean spirit, and packs a protein wallop, too. For all its sophistication, it is what I call "shovel food": for when you've been working your butt off all day and just need to shovel in some nourishment.

SERVES 2

Extra-virgin olive oil

8 oz/227 g ground lamb

¼ tsp fennel seeds

1 tbsp/9 g garlic, minced

½ recipe Lentil Doll (page 214), curry and peppercorns omitted

1 cup/160 g Marinated Tomato (page 217)

12 oz/340 g Fresh Pasta (page 64), formed into a wide cut of linguine

1½ cups/120 g fresh parsley, chopped

3 tbsp/43 g butter

Salt

Coarsely ground black pepper

Place ¼ inch/6 mm of olive oil in a Dutch oven or heavy, nonreactive saucepan over medium heat. When the oil is hot, add the lamb. Sauté, breaking it apart, until cooked through, about 5 minutes. Add the fennel seeds and garlic and cook for 2 more minutes. Then add the lentils and tomato. Let simmer for 20 minutes.

Cook the pasta according to the pasta recipe directions. Drain and toss with olive oil.

Make sure the lentil mixture is heated through. Add a bit of water if it's dry, but not too much. You want sauce, not soup. Stir in the parsley, then add the butter. As you mix in the butter, you will see the sauce emulsify, thicken a bit and become generally more saucy. (Tastier, too.) Season with salt and pepper.

Put the noodles on a heated platter, and spoon the lentil mixture over. Drizzle with more olive oil than is really prudent.

OLD BLEU

This used to be called Gnu Bleu, until it wasn't new anymore. At one point I tried to take it off the menu. There was howling. Banshees and zombies screaming at me walking down the street. Usually when we give a customer favorite a well-deserved rest, we continue to make it for those who continue to order it, but in this case I was told, "There are people who haven't had it. You need it on the menu." It's still there.

People who hate blue cheese love this dish. People who love blue cheese can't help having this over and over.

SERVES 1

---

1 cup/30 g loosely packed spinach

1 tbsp/15 ml olive oil

1 Roma tomato

Salt

2 basil leaves

¾ cup/177 ml heavy cream

2 oz/57 g crumbled blue cheese

6 oz/171 g Fresh Pasta (page 64), formed into pappardelle, or store-bought pappardelle

Heat up your broiler. Toss the spinach with the olive oil and set aside. Quarter the tomato. Rub it with oil and sprinkle it with salt. Place the tomato under the broiler until browned well and a little charred, and the texture of the interior is a little mushy. This will take less than 10 minutes. It might be a lot less. Broilers are the most variable cooking method there is, next to fire. When the tomatoes are done, turn off the broiler. Add the spinach and basil to the tomato and return to the still-warm oven to wilt the spinach.

Place the cream and blue cheese in a 12-inch/30 cm heavy-bottomed pan over medium heat. Get it bubbling, and reduce the volume until it is a sauce consistency, around 5 minutes. At this point the sauce can be held for a while, refrigerated or at room temperature.

Cook the pasta in boiling water according to pasta recipe or package directions. Toss with the sauce, turn onto a platter and top with the tomato mixture.

ONE MORE TIME

In the summer of 2009 I put "Pasta with Seared Scallops, Cured Peppered Beef, Caramelized Onion, Basil, Marsala Cream" on the menu. Cured beef, you ask? OK, pastrami. Red. If I called it pastrami, no one would buy it. But sweet scallops combine in a surprising and wonderful way with the salty beef, and our customers couldn't get enough. It was so popular that the chefs finally forced me to take it off the menu so they could make something else for a change. This is a great one for impressing your dinner-party guests, and it stands up to a nice medium-bodied red.

Overcooking is the ruination of scallops. Here they are seared on just one side so they get great flavor without becoming pencil erasers.

SERVES 2

10 oz/283 g Fresh Pasta (page 64)
¼ cup/60 ml olive oil, plus extra
12 oz/340 g Maine sea scallops
1 red onion, sliced
2 cloves garlic, minced
4 oz/113 g red pastrami, sliced thinly
3 tbsp/45 ml dry marsala wine
¾ cup/177 ml heavy cream
4 leaves basil
2 tbsp/10 g fresh parsley, chopped
Coarsely ground black pepper

Cook the pasta to al dente according to the pasta recipe directions. Drain it and toss with a little olive oil. Set aside.

Heat a 12-inch/30 cm skillet over medium-high heat. Brush the flat side of the scallops with a little oil, just enough for a light coat. Place them oiled side down in the pan. Let them sear and caramelize on that side for 4 minutes, then transfer them to a room-temperature plate.

In the same pan, pour the ¼ cup/60 ml of oil. Sauté the onion until sweet and translucent, about 5 minutes. Add the garlic and pastrami and brown the lot, another 7 minutes.

Remove from the heat and let it calm down. After a couple of minutes, add the marsala and cream. Return to the heat to reduce the sauce until it can coat a spoon. Toss in the basil and pasta.

Plate on a warm serving dish. Place the scallops on the pasta, seared side up, and dump any juice from the scallop plate onto the pasta. Finish with the Elvis Parsley, pepper and a drizzle of a fruity olive oil.

CONNIE'S, OLD SCHOOL

This is another "We are hungry, Nanna!" dish from my grandmother, Connie. It's easy, fast, uses leftover noodles, is filling and has tons of flavor. The best of peasant food: bowties with bacon, egg, spinach, caramelized onion, cheese and tomato.

SERVES 2

Olive oil

½ lb/227 g farfalle pasta (bowties, if you're not being fancy), cooked and cooled

4 oz/113 g uncooked thick-cut bacon, chopped up

1 cup/132 g red onion, sliced

2 tbsp/18 g garlic, minced

2 large eggs, broken into a small bowl

2 cups/60 g spinach, stemmed if needed

⅔ cup/106 g Marinated Tomato (page 217), diced

½ cup/88 g Romano cheese, shredded

Coarsely ground black pepper

Have a warm platter ready.

Heat a sauté pan (at least 12 inches/30 cm) over medium-high heat. Heat enough oil to just film the bottom. Add the bacon and onion. Sauté to sweat the onion and cook the bacon, browning both together, 5 to 7 minutes. Once the onion is soft and it's all nice and brown, push the mixture to the far edge of the pan. Add the garlic and stir.

Tilt the pan so the oil runs toward the handle. Slide the eggs into the oil and stir vigorously with a pair of tongs to scramble them. It will be quick! Add the spinach to the bacon mixture and stir, then add the pasta. Toss it all together. Let it heat, tossing from time to time to help it along. When hot through, turn out onto the platter. Place the tomato on one side of the pile and sprinkle it all with Romano. Serve with a pepper grinder.

Try to eat this slowly. I dare you.

P.M.S. (PASTA/ MUSSELS/SAUSAGE)

Roasted mussels must be one of the best things ever. And when did sausage not make the best things even better? If you have some pasta and sauce on hand, you can pick up the bivalves and sausage on your way home and have a quick, wonderful dinner.

SERVES 2

2 links Italian sausage

2½ cups/591 ml Latex Marinara (page 218)

½ lb/227 g mussels, washed and debearded, tossed in olive oil

4 sprigs oregano

12 oz/340 g Fresh Pasta (page 64), formed into linguine, or store-bought linguine

Preheat your oven to 450°F/232°C. Boil a big pot of salted water.

Put the sausages in an oven-safe casserole dish, 9 x 12 inches/23 x 30 cm or thereabouts, preferably metal. Put in the oven and roast until brown, 8 minutes or so. Remove the pan from the oven and let the sausages stop frying and relax. Once you can handle them, cut each sausage into at least 6 random pieces. It's OK if the sausage isn't cooked through because it's going back in the oven in a minute. The idea here is to brown the outside and have juiciness left so the sausage can poach along with the mussels.

Add the sauce, mussels and oregano to the casserole. Return to the oven. Put the pasta in the boiling water and cook to al dente, then drain and toss with a bit of olive oil.

The stuff in the oven is done when the mussels open, 8 to 12 minutes.

Put the noodles on a warm platter. Spoon the mussel mixture over it.

Serve with some Pellegrino, no lemon, no ice. Or a coarse red wine from the southern Italian coast or islands. Mmmmm.

SIMPLY DELISH

This buttery pasta highlights our native crabmeat, and works great with lobster, too. Simply Delish is a perennial summer favorite for our seasonal guests, and then we get complaints from the locals when it goes away for winter.

Of course Grandma Connie is looking down at this saying, *"MARRONE! Non formaggi con pesce!"*

SERVES 2

12 oz/340 g Fresh Pasta (page 64), or 9 oz/340 g dried whole wheat pasta

¾ cup/167 g (1½ sticks) butter! (you can eat rice cakes tomorrow)

10 oz/283 g Maine crab or lobster meat, chilled

6 tbsp/90 ml decent white wine

⅓ cup/33 g scallions, sliced on the bias

4 oz/113 g ricotta salata, shaved

2 tbsp/30 ml extra-virgin olive oil

½ lemon

Coarse salt

Plenty of coarsely ground black pepper

Cook the pasta according to the pasta recipe or package directions, then drain it and toss with a little olive oil.

In a heavy 10- to 12-inch/25.5 to 30 cm sauté pan (I prefer All-Clad stainless), over medium to high heat, melt the butter. Let it begin to brown. Aim for the color of a cardboard box. It's hard to say how long this will take. Times will vary with the pan thickness and so on. Suffice it to say that if you are still in this step 20 minutes from now, turn it up. When it starts getting there, a nutty, savory smell will fill your kitchen and the butter will begin to separate. Remove from the heat.

Lower the heat to medium-low. Return the pan to the burner and add the chilled crabmeat, which will stop the browning process before it gets out of hand. Add the wine. Be careful; it can splash and flame, just like on the tee-vee.

Sauté for 1 or 2 minutes, until the crabmeat is hot (at least 150°F/66°F). Treat the product tenderly; you don't want to break it up.

Add the scallions, then the pasta and toss it all together.

Plate on warmed dishes. Cheese it. Drizzle some nice fruity extra-virgin olive oil on top. Squeeze the lemon. Sprinkle with coarse salt and lotsa pepper.

CHEF'S TIP: If you can get a quality whole wheat pasta (what we call "dirt noodle," because it looks that way), this may be the only dish ever that it is good in. The nuttiness of the whole wheat really is of use here and a fine complement to the nuttiness of the brown butter.

WHADDYAGOT

This meal got made one day when I'd been up at five a.m. to walk the dog and do farm chores, then shed my Carhartts and muck boots for a sport coat and city shoes. I headed to Portland for a fancy event, then drove home, put on my Carhartts, got on the tractor and mowed around the garden. It was a full-circle day, and one that built up an appetite. I put a fire in the woodstove and raided the garden (sorry, Farmer Anne). This is "whaddyagot" pasta: garlic, onion, olive oil and whatever's growing. It's a live-in-the-moment dish that's equally at home in the city or the country.

SERVES 2

Small bunch of Swiss chard
2 Italian frying peppers
⅔ lb/300 g dried rigatoni pasta
½ cup/120 ml olive oil
½ cup/66 g Walla Walla onion, sliced
4 cloves garlic, smashed and chopped roughly
3 slices prosciutto, cut into strips
1 tomato, cut into big chunks
10 leaves basil

Boil a large pot of salted water.

Wash the chard and remove the stems. Cut the stalks on the bias into thin slices. Rip the leaves into bite-size chunks. Seed the peppers and tear them into big bites as well.

When the water boils, add the rigatoni and cook according to the package directions. Please do not overcook. Drain.

Place a heavy 12-inch/30 cm skillet over high heat. Wait until it is almost smoking, then carefully pour in the oil. Quickly add the onion. Splatter alert! Stir, then let cook until translucent, 5 minutes.

Add the garlic and sauté for about 2 minutes. When it smells awesome, add the peppers, prosciutto and chard stems. Sauté until the peppers' color intensifies and the texture relaxes, 3 to 4 minutes. Then add the chard leaves and tomato. Sauté for about 2 minutes more. The chard needs to wilt and get that smoooooth texture.

Add the basil and pasta; toss it all together. Plate on a warmed platter.

Grab the chilled Pellegrino (no ice) and a friend. *Mangia.*

SORTA LASAGNE

I love lasagne. However: the layering, the eggs, the mess, the unused noodles I am forced to eat up (with butter), ACK! So this is a deconstructed, or partially deconstructed and then reassembled, version. All the good stuff, none of the ACK!

SERVES 1

1 cup/237 ml Latex Marinara (page 218)

1 (8" x 8"/20 x 20 cm) sheet of Fresh Pasta (page 64)

Extra-virgin olive oil

5 oz/142 g ricotta cheese

⅓ cup/57 g Romano or Parmesan cheese, grated

3 leaves basil

3 oz/85 g mozzarella cheese, shredded

1 cup/30 g spinach or greens of choice, stemmed and oiled

Cook the pasta to al dente. Drain, let cool, then toss in olive oil.

Preheat your oven to 400°F/204°C.

In a 7- to 9-inch/18 to 23 cm oven-safe casserole dish, place half of the marinara. Put in the sheet of pasta so that half of it (a triangle shape) is in the casserole, and the other corner is hanging out.

On the fat part of the triangle in the casserole, place the ricotta, half of the Romano and the basil leaves. Fold over the pasta so the corners match up. Press on the pasta to squish the filling to distribute it, but not quite all the way to the edges of the pasta.

Top with the remaining marinara, then the mozzarella and the remaining Romano. Bake until bubbling, browned and hot throughout, around 40 minutes. Add the spinach and return to the oven for a couple of minutes, to wilt.

Do not burn your mouth. Patience.

Eat with some cheap red wine in a box. Shovel 'n swill.

SPAGHETTI WIT

Wit meatballs, that is. This is the only dish to have survived every menu change for all these years. My interest in food, the café and this here book can all be traced back to my grandma's plates of spaghetti, sauce and meatballs. Forget towers of whatever, drizzles and smears; this is FOOD, absent ego, all heart.

This dish is a home run for any occasion. Scale it up to feed a bunch of loud Italian Americans, or enjoy a quiet-time dinner with the one you adore, with Chianti in the basket.

SERVES 2

4 to 8 Nanna Connie's Meatballs (recipe follows)

3 cups/710 ml Latex Marinara (page 218)

14 oz/397 g Fresh Pasta (page 64), formed into linguine (Yes, I am aware that it's supposed to be spaghetti. This is the cut Nanna Connie used. YOU argue with her in the afterlife.)

Olive oil

½ cup/85 g Romano or Parmesan cheese, freshly grated

Parsley, to garnish

Hot pepper flakes

Place the meatballs over medium heat in a medium saucepan. Add the sauce and heat so that it gets moving. Just as the sauce begins to bubble, lower the heat as low as it will go. Simmer for 10 to 15 minutes, until the meatballs are heated through. Longer won't hurt, and the sauce will get infused with meatbally flavor. Just stir it from time to time and add water if it thickens up too much.

Cook the pasta according to the pasta recipe directions. Drain and toss in a little oil. Place the noodles on a heated platter. Spoon the meatballs around the edges of the linguine. Pour the sauce in a stripe down the middle. Sprinkle the cheese all around, top with parsley and serve with some hot pepper flakes on the side.

Get that Chianti in the basket. Eat up!

NANNA CONNIE'S MEATBALLS

I think these are best understood as "meat truffles." Combined with sauce and pasta they make Spaghetti Wit, my ultimate comfort food.

As kids, my brother and I would drop in on Nanna Connie, Auntie Fluffie and our cousins Frank and Kathy, conveniently located next door. We'd grab a couple un-sauced meatballs out of the fridge, sprinkle with salt and eat. The best.

Connie passed away early in my cooking career, and the exact recipe left our earth with her. I had to do some forensic recipe research. Oh, did I try to get it just right. After exhausting mixing, cooking and eating of many batches (chilling some to look for the exact taste and texture I remember from those refrigerator meatballs), I had my cousin Kathy give me her opinion. "OK," said Kathy. Bingo.

MAKES ABOUT TWENTY 2-OUNCE/57 G MEATBALLS

1¼ cups/251 g onion, minced

½ cup/60 g celery, minced

3 tbsp/27 g garlic, minced

3 tbsp/45 ml olive oil, plus more for frying

½ lb/227 g ground pork

½ lb/227 g ground veal

⅔ cup/80 g Romano cheese, ground

3 tbsp/15 g fresh parsley, minced

3 large eggs

⅓ cup/40 g unseasoned bread crumbs

1 tsp salt

2½ tsp/6 g coarsely ground black pepper

Choose a pan that is heavy and more broad than tall. A 12-inch/30 cm straight-sided sauté pan is perfect. Put in the onion, celery, garlic and the 3 tbsp/45 ml of olive oil. Cook over medium heat to sweat them; that is, let them get soft and sweet, about 10 minutes. Remove from the heat and chill.

Once cold, mix the vegetables with all the remaining ingredients. Shape the mixture into 2-ounce/57 g balls, about 2 inches/5 cm in diameter.

Put an inch/2.5 cm of olive oil into a 12-inch/30 cm cast-iron skillet. Heat over medium heat to 350°F/177°C. Fry the meatballs in batches, browning well all over, 8 to 10 minutes per batch. As each batch finishes, transfer it to paper towels to drain. I dare you not to eat at least one!

Once cooked, these will keep in the refrigerator for about 4 days. They also freeze well.

To eat, simmer in tomato sauce, or just eat them as they are, chilled, with salt.

4

VEGETABLES AND SIDES

When I was a vegetarian in the '70s, and eating way too much beans and rice to sustain basic happiness, I asked my Nanna Connie to teach me about cooking vegetables. She had a hard time understanding what I was getting at. "No meat?" she said. "Really?" But then she showed me some Lenten dishes from the Old World. Her vegetables were fresh, warm, salty and wonderful: the kind of robust peasant food that inspired my restaurant.

This chapter includes recipes that bring out the fantastic flavors and textures of vegetables. The Oven-Roasted Kale is a perennial favorite, sweetened by roasted onions and balsamic vinegar, perked up with cheese, softened by mushrooms. It goes with everything. You'll also find a variety of vegetables in rich sauces that you can serve as a meal on their own: Green Beans in Yellow Curry, It's Spring Somewhere (a creamy asparagus dish) and, of course, Brussels Sprouts, which beat out even the kale for most popular vegetable at our restaurant (really). This chapter also includes some lighter, fresher vegetable preparations, like the Roasted Ear of Corn, and The Usual Suspects, which is the slaw of cabbage, lime and cilantro that accompanies about half of the dishes we ever serve.

As much as I love vegetables, there's a special place in my heart for starches—delicious, creamy, toasty, comforting starches. Look in this chapter for perfect All-Purpose Mashed Potatoes and foolproof French fries, as well as Polenta and Risotto for those days when you want to impress someone who doesn't know how easy these actually are to make.

OVEN-ROASTED KALE

When I worked at the East Wind Inn in the late 1980s, Pat Patterson used to come by and offer up his garden vegetables. He asked if we could use some kale; he had to mow it down with a bush hog to keep it under control. One day, having forgotten to make a vegetable to serve with a steak, I tossed some greens with olive oil and threw them in the oven. The result was so good that I told Pat I'd take all the greens off his hands, and the roasted greens have become a signature side.

Now, we're growing our own kale and chard at Headacre Farm, but have yet to reach Pat's levels of production. The bush hog is ready just in case.

This is a versatile dish that can be served hot, cold or at room temperature. With poached eggs and some bread it makes a vegetarian meal for two. It's excellent as a side, too, or heaped in a dish on a party buffet.

SERVES 4 AS A SIDE

½ lb/227 g kale
¼ cup/60 ml olive oil
9 medium mushrooms
1 medium red onion, sliced thinly
2 cloves garlic, minced
2 oz/57 g feta cheese, crumbled
1 tbsp/15 ml balsamic vinegar
¼ tsp coarse salt
Coarsely ground black pepper

Place a rack in the lowest position of the oven and preheat to 500°F/260°C. If you are planning to serve hot, have ready a warm platter.

Remove the stems from the kale and rip the leaves into 3-inch/8 cm pieces. Wash the leaves and dry well in a salad spinner or with towels.

Drizzle 1 tablespoon/15 ml of the olive oil over the leaves and toss until thoroughly coated. At this point you can put the greens in a sealed container and refrigerate them for several days. The oil will prevent spoilage and tenderize the greens at the same time.

Whack the mushrooms: Place each on a cutting board and hit it hard with the flat of your hand. If there are children around, give them a turn. Then send them out of the kitchen because it is about to get hot.

On your heaviest cookie sheet, toss the onion and mushrooms with 2 tablespoons/ 30 ml of the olive oil. Put the sheet in the oven on the lowest rack. Every 4 or 5 minutes, use your tongs to move the vegetables around and flip the mushrooms. When the onion starts to turn brown, after 8 or 10 minutes, add the garlic. The onion should be cooked through and soft within another minute or two. Take the vegetables out of the oven and remove them from the pan.

Spread the kale on the empty cookie sheet so that there is minimal overlap. Place on the bottom rack and switch the oven to the broiler setting. Now you need to be vigilant. Don't step away from your oven. Once a minute, open the oven and attack the kale with your tongs, moving the leaves around and flipping them over. After 5 or 6 minutes, the kale will become darker and some parts will begin to char. Return the rest of the vegetables to the pan to reheat them for a couple of minutes.

Dump the vegetables onto a platter, and drizzle with the remaining tablespoon/ 15 ml of olive oil (this is a time to use your good stuff). Sprinkle on the feta, vinegar, salt and several grinds of pepper. Toss a few times and serve.

GRILLED RADICCHIO

Sienna, Italy, 1994. In an out-of-the-way tavern, I peered through the glass into the kitchen, where commotion seemed to be the norm. Through the chaos I saw an expansive char grill, which was cooking . . . was that radicchio? Lettuce! On a grill! Had they lost their mind?

In 1994 we did not say OMG, but: OMG. It was delicious! The bitter-edged leaves, appreciated in a salad, became a supple, full-flavored, rich vegetable. So weird, so gooooood!

SERVES 2

---

1 medium head radicchio, quartered

Good olive oil, a lot

3 tbsp/45 ml fine balsamic vinegar

4 oz/113 g ricotta salata

Coarse salt

Coarsely ground black pepper

½ handful of pine nuts, toasted

For this you will need a charcoal or gas grill. Get the fire going and build up an even heat over a medium-high flame.

Saturate the radicchio in the olive oil. Make sure it gets into all those deep recesses. Drain off the excess.

Place the radicchio on the grill, flat side down. A little char is fine, but keep an eye on it; you may need to turn down your flame. Brush occasionally with more olive oil, and turn the wedges so they cook on all 3 sides. Your goal is for the heat to penetrate all the way through the radicchio, and you don't want to char the heck out of it. A lot will depend on your grill, but as a ballpark this will take 4 to 5 minutes on each side. Cook until the entire lettuce is heated through. The color will deepen and the white spines will become more opaque.

Place the radicchio, pointy side up, on a warm platter. Drizzle the balsamic over, and sprinkle the cheese. Pour on yet more olive oil, and scatter over a good amount of coarse salt and some pepper. Sprinkle the pine nuts about.

Serve with a house red in a teeny flat-bottomed glass. Put soccer on the TV. *Mangia.*

GREEN BEANS IN YELLOW CURRY

Spicy, crunchy, slurpy and easy! There's enough sauce here to make it a little bit like soup, but the focus is on the green beans. It makes a nice first course or a luncheon entrée.

SERVES 2 AS AN APPETIZER

Vegetable oil

1 tbsp/15 ml yellow Thai curry paste

3 oz/85 ml vegetable stock

4 oz/113 ml coconut milk

8 to 12 green beans, ends snipped off

½ red sweet pepper, seeded and ripped into 1"/2.5 cm chunks

A few leaves basil

1 tsp garlic, minced

1 tsp fresh ginger, minced

1 tsp Thai fish sauce

1 oz/28 g mung bean sprouts

2 scallions, white and green parts, sliced on the bias

3 sprigs cilantro

Lime wedge

½ tsp black sesame seeds

In a heavy 4-quart/4 L saucepan on medium heat, place enough oil to coat the bottom. Add the curry paste and sauté, stirring, to develop flavor. What an aroma! After about 30 seconds, add the stock and coconut milk. Bring to a boil, then reduce to a simmer.

Add the beans and red pepper. Cook for 1 minute, then cover, remove from the heat, and let sit for 2 minutes. Stir in the basil, garlic, ginger and fish sauce.

Pour the contents of the pot into a heated bowl. Top with the mung bean sprouts, scallions and cilantro. Squeeze the lime and sprinkle the black sesame seeds.

IT'S SPRING SOMEWHERE

At the restaurant we sometimes call this "Asparagus Debris" because it is asparagus, cooked with . . . Brie. And cream, of course! This is rich but bursting with the vitality of spring, even when it is November and you are buying asparagus from another hemisphere.

SERVES 1 TO 2

---

10 stalks asparagus
¼ cup/60 ml extra-virgin olive oil
½ red sweet pepper, ripped coarsely
¼ red onion, sliced
2 cloves garlic, minced
2 oz/57 g Brie cheese
6 tbsp/90 ml heavy cream
2 tbsp/10 g fresh parsley, coarsely chopped

Prepare the asparagus: Bend the stalks near the bottom until the tough part breaks off. Discard the tough parts (or make soup out of them).

Heat a heavy 10- to 12-inch/25.5 to 30 cm skillet over medium to high heat. Pour in olive oil to coat the pan. Add the red pepper and onion and sauté until you smell the goodness and see the color intensify, 5 minutes. Toss in the asparagus and sauté. As soon as the color starts changing, add the garlic. Cook for about 1 minute.

Turn down the heat to medium. Add the chunk of Brie and the cream. The Brie will begin to melt and bind with the cream. Do not stir, as you want the cheese to hold its own and you want to reduce the cream.

When the cream has thickened a bit (after about 5 minutes), add the parsley and remove from the heat.

Turn out onto a heated platter. Dress with more extra-virgin olive oil.

ROASTED BEETS

Beets come in a variety of colors, and any type will do here. I do like the standard red that Farmer Anne grows here at Headacre Farm. As with any root vegetable, low and slow cooking is the best way to heighten the flavor by converting starches into sugars. Here we simmer the beets in flavored water first, which helps with the peeling.

SERVES 2

4 tennis ball–size beets, or equivalent

2 bay leaves

10 black peppercorns

2 cloves garlic

¾ cup/99 g red onion, sliced

Extra-virgin olive oil

Salt

¼ cup/60 ml chicken or vegetable stock

4 tsp/12 g garlic, minced

2 tbsp/30 ml balsamic vinegar

2 tsp/10 g prepared horseradish (preferably Morse's brand)

2 tbsp/10 g fresh parsley, chopped

2 tbsp/28 g butter

Salt

Coarsely ground black pepper

Preheat your oven to 375°F/191°C.

Find a pot deep enough that you can cover the beets with at least an inch/2.5 cm of water. Put in the beets, bay leaves, peppercorns, garlic, ¼ cup/33 g of the onion and the aforementioned water. Add a good pinch of salt. Bring to a boil, then lower the heat to a simmer. Cover and simmer until tender, about 45 minutes. Drain and cool until you can handle the beets, then peel. Cut into 2-inch/5 cm chunks.

In a bowl, combine the cut beets with the remaining onion. Toss with olive oil. Spread the mixture in a 9 x 12-inch/23 x 30 cm oven-safe casserole dish and put it in the oven. Roast for about 10 minutes, until you see the onion browning and the beets developing a sort of crust (the color will change). Remove from the oven and add the stock, garlic, balsamic and horseradish. Sprinkle with the parsley and swirl in the butter. Sprinkle with salt and grind some pepper. Dump it all out on a heated platter.

Purple lips will soon be yours.

SHIITAKES HAVE HIT THE FAN

We have a vintage fan on the counter to circulate the air in the kitchen by the brick oven. On a whim one night, I tossed a shiitake at the fan. As might have been expected, the blades sliced it up and sprayed mushroom all over the customers. It was a dumb thing to do, but we got a good story and a good name for a dish out of it.

This is a supertasty appetizer, with the meatiness of mushrooms and the richness of a marsala cream sauce. Serve it with a dry white wine and focaccia for mopping up every bit of the sauce.

SERVES 2

10 shiitake mushrooms, stemmed
¼ cup/33 g red onion, sliced
1 tbsp/15 ml butter
1 tbsp/15 ml olive oil
1 tsp garlic, minced
1 cup/30 g greens (this is good with frisée)
1 tbsp/15 ml dry marsala wine
½ cup/118 ml heavy cream
1 sprig French tarragon
Salt
Coarsely ground black pepper

Preheat your oven to 400°F/204°C.

In a 10-inch/25.5 cm round or 9 x 12-inch/23 x 30 cm oven-safe casserole dish, place the mushrooms, onion, butter and olive oil. Roast, stirring for even browning. When the onion is nice and brown, after about 5 minutes, remove the dish from the oven. Stir in the garlic and add the greens, stirring to coat with the fat and the good stuff. Add the marsala, cream and tarragon. Return to the oven.

Now your stovetop is free to make the main course! The greens will be roasting and the cream thickening. You want it to coat a spoon, which should take about 4 minutes. Once it has thickened, remove from the oven and season with salt.

Pour the mixture into a heated flat-bottomed bowl. Grind a liberal amount of black pepper over it. Pop the cork.

CHEF'S TIP: I hate wasting anything, and for years I have tried to find a use for shiitake stems. They really shouldn't go in this dish. But I suggest cooking the hell out of them and mincing them up to add into your next veggie stock.

THE USUAL SUSPECTS

This is a multiuse item. Its inspiration is "flavors of where it is hot outside." That would not usually be Maine, unless it's that one day in the summer. We don't care what the temperature is; we still want to eat great hot-weather food. This slaw works as Mexican, Southeast Asian or whenever you need a bright crunch of lime, salt and cilantro. It's called The Usual Suspects because we call on it so often.

MAKES 1¼ CUPS/420 G

1½ cups/500 g thinly shredded napa cabbage

6 sprigs cilantro

2 tsp/10 g black sesame seeds

Juice of 1 lime

2 tsp/10 ml Thai fish sauce

¼ cup/33 g red onion, sliced as thinly as you can

Mix all the ingredients. Eat.

The slaw can be made as you need it, or kept for a day or two. If you make it ahead, its character will change; think of it as more of a marinated vegetable.

CHEF'S TIP: This is a fat-free dish. Odd for a Cafe Miranda recipe? Really, no. We often use this as a counterpoint to heavy dishes (coconut milk curries, burritos, fried chicken). For a light summer meal, see Shrimp, Avocado and The Usual Suspects (page 47). You can easily make this vegan by using a vegetarian "fish" sauce—it will be different, but good.

BRUSSELS SPROUTS: THE DISREGARDED VEGETABLE

"What? *No Brussels sprouts!?*" say our customers, every spring. As asparagus and fiddleheads appear, we dump from the menu all the winter foods we are tired of: brown stocks, sausages, braises, cabbages and Brussels sprouts. At least, we try. But, for you? Here it is for any time the mini cabbages are available!

Cooking Brussels sprouts in cream makes an asset of the bitterness that is so often a turnoff. These are sweet and creamy with just enough of that bitter edge to keep you gobbling them down. Are these better with bacon? Yes. Is bacon necessary? Not at all.

SERVES 2

1 lb/454 g Brussels sprouts

½ cup/66 g red onion, sliced

¼ cup/60 ml olive oil, plus a little more

2 cloves garlic, chopped coarsely

7 medium button mushrooms, smashed

2 oz/56 g uncooked thick-cut bacon, chopped into pinky-size pieces (optional)

1 tbsp/15 ml balsamic vinegar

6 tbsp/89 ml heavy cream

Pinch salt

Coarsely ground black pepper

Chopped fresh parsley, to finish

Preheat your oven to 450°F/232°C.

Cut off the bottom (the brown part) of each sprout. Quarter them and toss with a little olive oil to coat.

In a heavy 11-inch/28 cm round (or equivalent in surface area) oven-safe casserole dish or skillet, place the sprouts, onion, garlic, mushrooms, bacon (if using) and the ¼ cup/60 ml of olive oil. Put it in the oven and roast, stirring occasionally, until everything is browned well. Depending on your pan and your oven, this can take upward of 25 minutes.

When the sprouts are just getting tender, carefully add the vinegar. Add the cream, then continue roasting.

Let the liquid reduce until it is thick enough to coat a spoon, about 8 minutes. Serve in the pan (careful of the Formica) or on a nice platter. Add salt, a grinding of pepper and an Elvis Parsley sprinkle.

ROASTED EAR OF CORN

Mexican street food inspired this dish. Down there, you can get a roasted ear of somewhat tough corn, dredged in your choice of coarse sugar or ground dried chiles. Our version isn't anything like that, of course. We take the idea of sharp, punchy seasonings in a different direction and cover our corn with a sweet and spicy Sriracha-butter sauce. On the side is a pile of crunchy, fresh slaw, and lime wedges give it all a burst of brightness. You will want to have plenty of napkins on hand.

This dish is best with sweet late-summer corn. We get ours from Weskeag Farms, just over the hill from our own Headacre.

SERVES 2

2 ears corn

Vegetable oil

Coarse salt

4 tbsp/57 g (½ stick) butter

2 tbsp/30 ml Sriracha, plus more to finish

2 tsp/10 ml sweet chili sauce (we use Mae Ploy brand)

½ cup/170 g The Usual Suspects (page 101)

2 lime wedges

Shuck the corn, but leave the husks attached. Bend the husks around the butt end. Take a leaf off and tie them back, all together. Remove the hairlike corn silk. Fire up your broiler and place the rack in the middle. If you have a bottom broiler, the corn will be closer to the fire, so you'll have to keep a real close eye on it.

Brush the corn with oil, just to coat. Sprinkle it with salt. Place on a sheet pan or cookie sheet. Into the broiler! This requires constant vigilance. Let the corn brown, turning so that it cooks evenly. When browned all over, about 8 minutes total, remove from the oven.

Place the butter in the pan and slide it around to melt. Add the 2 tablespoons/30 ml of Sriracha and chili sauce and stir.

Place the corn on a warm platter. Pour the sauce over. Put 2 piles of The Usual Suspects at opposite ends of the plate. Serve with lime wedges on the side, and drizzle additional Sriracha around for show.

MIRANDAKIMCHI

We often make a version of kimchi to serve with steaks, scallops, tuna and other grilled or steamed proteins (tofu is a great match). We follow the spirit rather than the letter of the kimchi tradition, using what is locally available and preserving it for the cold months. Sometimes we fill the crock with a variety of leafy greens, such as bok choy and kale, or Brussels sprouts and other cabbagey things, even zucchini or radishes. Napa cabbage is the baseline, and that's what I describe here. It's simple to do—you mix it up, crock it and let it ferment for a while (and by "a while" I mean over a week, so be prepared). We do not dig the traditional hole in the ground, but you could (and, if you're bothered by the aroma, maybe you'll want to).

MAKES ABOUT 4 CUPS/945 ML

---

1 head napa cabbage (about 1½ lb/680 g), sliced ½"/1.5 cm thick

12 radishes, shredded

3 cloves garlic, chopped coarsely

3 tbsp/18 g dried kimchi flakes (Asian grocery time!)

1 bunch scallions, chopped

6 tbsp/90 ml freshly squeezed lime juice

4 tbsp/60 ml Thai fish sauce

½ cup/40 g cilantro, chopped like you hate it

Combine all and mix well. Place in a 6-quart/6 L nonmetal, nonreactive crock with a cover. Make sure there is some headroom for expansion. Place a plate on the top of the mixture; this will keep all submerged in the liquid. Do this or nasty mold will appear. The cover shouldn't be airtight. The gas that is produced by the fermentation needs to be able to get out.

Dig. Oh, kidding!

Place in your fridge for a couple of weeks. Yes, that long. However, I recommend eating some of this fresh, as a delicious, spicy slaw.

It will bubble. It's alive!

Scoop it out as needed. You can leave this in the refrigerator for a good while. The flavor will continue to strengthen. It is closest to traditional kimchi after about 2 weeks, but good at any stage.

ALL-PURPOSE MASHED POTATOES WITH GARLIC

We use these everywhere. Once made and chilled they reheat wonderfully! Make a full batch. They won't last.

These are best if you use a starch potato, not a water potato. You can tell the difference by the shape: Starch spuds are oblong and water potatoes are usually roundish. Russets are a good bet.

SERVES 2

4 medium spuds, cut into large dice

½ cup/66 g onion, sliced

2 whole cloves garlic, plus 2 cloves, minced

1 bay leaf

¼ cup/57 g (½ stick) butter

¼ cup/60 ml heavy cream

¼ cup/60 ml whole milk

Salt

Coarsely ground black pepper

Put the potatoes in a pot that will hold them all with a little room. Add the onion, whole garlic cloves and bay leaf. Cover with cold water to cover by 2 inches/5 cm. Salt the water.

Bring to a boil over high heat, and then lower the heat so that the water simmers. Cook until the potatoes are tender when pierced with a fork, about 12 minutes. Drain. Return to the pot.

Add the butter, cream, milk and minced garlic. Mash. Now, don't use any kind of fancy mixer. An old-fashioned masher does the best job. Lumps are a sign of a dish "individually crafted by hand," so don't try too hard to get them all out. Add salt and pepper to taste.

At this point, you can refrigerate the potatoes for a few days. To reheat, microwave or bake along with whatever you'd like to serve them with. If the potatoes brown in the oven, all the better. They get way delish, like really good Tater Tots.

POLENTA

There are two ways to eat polenta. It can be served creamy, which for me brings back memories of Nanna Connie (and farina cereal). Or the soft polenta can be poured into a shallow tub, cooled until solid, sliced up and crisped up via skillet, deep fryer, grill or oven. This gives a delicious contrast of textures and flavors between the brown, crispy/chewy crust and the soft interior.

Soft polenta is delicious for breakfast with butter and maple syrup, or for dinner under a Bolognese sauce, eggs, greens . . . any number of yummy things. A slab of polenta makes an unusual and delicious accompaniment to a meal. It's a groovy side for a barbecue. It's also perfect for a gluten-free breakfast; try eggs Bennie, for example.

A double boiler makes this idiot-resistant. This doesn't require fancy equipment; you can just put a stainless-steel bowl over a pot of boiling water.

MAKES 5 CUPS/1340 GRAMS

4 cups/946 ml water
Salt
Coarsely ground black pepper
½ cup/112 g (1 stick) butter
1 bay leaf
1 cup/170 g cornmeal or grits

Heat the double boiler. In the top, place all the ingredients, except the cornmeal. Cover and cook until hot, just short of boiling, and all the butter is melted. Whisk in the cornmeal. Keep stirring with the whisk. Do not leave it. You will see and feel the mixture getting thicker. Keep stirring, paying attention that the bottom and corners of the pot are scraped. Do this until you feel that you're trying to stir cement, which will take at least 10 minutes. Cover and lower the heat so that the water is just barely simmering.

Ok, now you can leave it alone. Give it a half-hour on simmer. You can hold the soft version for an hour or so, adding liquid as needed. The consistency should be lavalike, not too loose or runny.

To make the firm version, pour the soft, hot polenta into a 9 x 12-inch/23 x 30 cm baking dish or similar shallow container. Let cool on a rack to room temperature, then refrigerate. At this point it will keep for 4 or 5 days.

To serve, slice the now-firm polenta into wedges or squares. Heat ½ inch/1.5 cm of oil in a skillet to 350°F/177°C. Fry on both sides until crisp, 5 minutes or so. You can also grill the squares (brush with oil first) or deep-fry them.

RISOTTO (THE CHEATER METHOD)

For a long time, risotto, was a "HTF do they make it?" dish. Who has the time? Then I had a life-changing risotto in Italy . . . at a truck stop on the Autostrade! If they could do it at a truck stop, I figured there was a chance I could pull it off. What I learned there is that a simple version is clear and memorable, so I use plain water rather than stock, to keep the flavor profile simple (you can use stock if you prefer). The cheater is that you par-cook a lot of it, then finish it quickly when it's needed. You can do these steps one after the other or days apart.

MAKES ABOUT 4 CUPS/640 G

6 tbsp/86 g butter
2 cups/400 g arborio rice
4 cups/946 ml water

Place the butter in a medium or large saucepan over medium heat. When it has melted, add the rice. Sauté slooooowwwwly, stirring, so that the rice does not brown. It will begin to turn opaque and absorb some of the butter.

Add just enough water to barely cover the rice. Lower the heat to medium-low; you want enough heat to help with absorption, but not so much that it boils or evaporates the water. Keep stirring. The rice has an outer jacket of soluble starch. The stirring frees some of that to produce the creamy goodness associated with risotto.

When the water is absorbed, add more water to barely cover the rice again. Repeat the process (stirring) until you have used up 2 cups/475 ml of the water.

At this point, you can finish the risotto by continuing to add water and stir until an additional 2 cups/475 ml of water has been absorbed.

Or, to use the cheater method, remove the half-cooked rice and spread it on a cookie sheet to cool. Once it is room temperature, store it in the refrigerator. When you want to serve the risotto, return it to the pot and continue the process with the remaining 2 cups/475 ml of water.

For a simple, tasty dish, stir in 3 ounces/85 g of grated Parmesan or Romano cheese. You can also add mushrooms, meats, seafood or vegetables to make a more substantial meal.

FRIES WITH THAT?

We've been making these fries for a long time and have perfected a recipe that has a creamy inside and crispy outside dusted in garlic and salt. Try them in a hash (page 200) or even in salad (page 43). Don't forget to see my tips for perfect fries, below.

SERVES 2 TO 3

---

4 russet or other starchy potatoes

Canola oil, for frying

¼ cup/20 g fresh parsley, coarsely chopped

1 tbsp/19 g garlic, minced

Table salt (Hold your fancy coarse stuff—this needs to be fine so it will stick.)

2 tbsp/30 ml olive oil

Cut the spuds into ½-inch/1.5 cm matchsticks. Place these apples of the earth in a big pot and run cold water over them. Stir to release the starches. When the water runs clear, drain and dry.

Fill your deep fryer with oil, or put enough to float the fries into a Dutch oven or other heavy pan. Heat it to 300°F/149°C. Add half of the potatoes. Cook until tender through-out, about 8 minutes (the time will vary according to how thickly you've cut them). Drain. Do the other half. Let cool to room temperature (or refrigerate for up to 2 days).

When you are ready to finish the fries, preheat your oven to 250°F/121°C. Put in a sheet pan to warm it up.

Place the parsley and garlic in a medium bowl.

In your deep fryer or a heavy pan, heat your fat to 325°F/163°C. Put in half of the fries and cook until they are well browned. Drain and spread on the sheet pan; keep warm in the oven. Drop in the second batch and brown them, too. Drain and put in the bowl with the parsley and garlic. Add the potato sticks from the oven along with more salt than you think is healthy, and the olive oil. Toss. Turn out on a heated platter and serve with a ketchuplike condiment. We use Heinz Chili Sauce, which is thinner than ketchup, with more vinegar and chunky onions. Malt vinegar or aioli would also be delicious.

> **CHEF'S TIPS:** There are a few keys to perfect fries. **First:** Get the right potato. You need a starchy variety, such as a russet or a Maine Shepody. The starchy types have an oval shape. Round ones are what I call water potatoes—they have less starch and more moisture, which makes browning difficult and gives a mealy texture. **Second:** You must cook them twice. The first frying uses oil at a cooler temperature, 300°F/149°C, to cook the potato through; the second is to brown and crisp the exterior. **Third:** Use clean oil. We prefer canola. **Fourth:** Temperature. It is crucial that in the second round, the fat temp does not go below 325°F/163°C. A deep fryer with a temperature gauge is handy; you can also use a large, heavy pot with a candy thermometer. Cook the potatoes in 2 batches; if you crowd the pot, the temperature will drop too much.

5

DINNERS

Here we are at the heart of it all. These dinner dishes are real food, hearty, life affirming. They are made of the best stuff we can get, prepared to make the most of it. This chapter includes your traditional meat and potatoes (Roast Chops with Apples, Bistro Job), as well as worldly treatments of local ingredients, like our Secret Scallops or Intergalactic Pork. Gnu Thing and Veg Wowie are vegetarian delights, and the Frittata and Huevos Miranda offer lighter options that will also work for a brunch. Every dish here is designed as a meal on its own, with no need for side dishes, though good bread and perhaps a salad seldom go amiss. The recipes are written for one or two people and ready to scale up, so you can make them for a weekday evening at home or a special-occasion party.

STEAKHOUSE

A few years ago I met up with some longtime pals in NYC and we went to a well-known steakhouse. Hunk-o-meat-o-rama! There was a vegetarian at the table; I won't go into details, but suffice it to say she is one no longer. The event is a bit fuzzy from the massive intake of protein, wine and martinis, but a Miranda favorite emerged from it.

Contrary to popular belief, classic American steakhouses do not use char grills. They use a box broiler, a piece of equipment that pros hate (brutally hot, unwieldy) but that does produce hard-to-beat steaks. For home cooking, the closest thing is the trusty cast-iron pan.

SERVES 1

2 tsp/1 g dried chervil

1 tsp garlic powder

1 tsp salt

1 tsp finely ground white pepper

12 oz/340 g New York sirloin strip, boneless

½ cup/118 ml heavy cream

1 tbsp/15 ml marsala wine

1 cup/30 g spinach, stemmed

Pinch freshly grated nutmeg

1 big, ripe heirloom tomato, sliced ¾"/2 cm thick

1 tbsp/15 ml balsamic vinegar

Coarsely ground black pepper

Coarse salt

Make a dry rub: Mix the chervil, garlic powder, salt and white pepper in a bowl. Rub the steak with it.

Place a 9-inch/23 cm cast-iron pan over high heat. I hope you have a good fan because the smoke detector will be ringing!

In a 2-quart/2 L saucepan over medium-high heat, place the cream and marsala. You are going to reduce it until half of the liquid has evaporated and the mixture is thick enough to coat a spoon, about 5 minutes. At this point hold it as is, parked, as it were.

Meanwhile, toss the steak on the hot pan: SMOKE! Good smells!

Sear one side. You will see the cooking action as the color moves up the side of the meat. When the color gets about one-third of the way up, flip the steak. Do the same for the other side, and that should take you to medium-rare. Remove from the pan.

Add the spinach and nutmeg to the cream and heat to wilt the leaves.

Place the tomato slices on the platter like shingles. Drizzle with balsamic and salt and pepper well. Pour the spinach mixture onto the plate. Place the steak in the center.

Serve with a baked potato and copious amounts of real butter and sour cream, for the full effect. Put your cardio surgeon on speed dial, pop a big cabernet, put on the hockey game and chow down.

CHEF'S TIP: Tell your butcher to get a "small eye" steak. This means that the entire strip is a smaller one so your steak will be thicker. A good thing.

BISTRO JOB

What makes a bistro a bistro? It is probably the steak frites. Classic meat and potatoes. Our response to this, menu-wise and wise-as-in-guy, is Bistro Job. It's both a nod and a smirk, the way we like it. It appeals to anybody: fries, greens (healthy!) and meat, along with a mushroomy, creamy, bluesy sauce. Can't miss!

A typical bistro would use a cut of steak that's a step below your rib eye or sirloin strip. Hanger steak, club, teres major, top sirloin, flank, London broil or the very cleverly named bistro steak will all work for this. Of course, feel free to go out and get the dry-aged Angus blah blah; can't hurt.

SERVES 2

Canola oil for, frying

3 good-size russet spuds, cut into fries that are ½"/1.5 cm thick (see notes on fries, page 34)

2 oz/30 ml Worcestershire sauce

Coarsely ground black pepper

2 tsp/10 ml freshly squeezed lemon juice

2 (10 oz/285 g) steaks (see headnote, or ask your butcher for suggestions)

¼ cup/60 ml extra-virgin olive oil

12 button mushrooms

¾ cup/177 ml beef stock

6 tbsp/89 ml heavy cream

4 oz/113 g blue cheese crumbles

2 cups/60 g arugula

2 tsp/6 g garlic, minced

Coarse salt

Heat your deep fryer or a heavy pan with canola oil to 300°F/149°C. Add the potatoes, in batches if necessary, and cook until tender, about 8 minutes. Drain and let cool.

Preheat your oven to 450°F/232°C. Mix the Worcestershire sauce, 1 tablespoon/7 g of the pepper and the lemon juice together and add the steaks. Let them marinate while you prepare the rest of the dish. Turn frequently so that the meat absorbs the flavors.

Toss the mushrooms in a bit of the olive oil. Place them in a 9-inch/23 cm cast-iron skillet or casserole dish. Roast until heated through, about 10 minutes. Add the stock, cream and blue cheese and return to the oven. Allow to cook until the sauce reduces and thickens enough to coat a spoon.

Heat a 9-inch/23 cm cast-iron skillet over medium-high heat. Heat your canola oil to 325°F/163°C.

Put the arugula in a large bowl along with the garlic and a splash of olive oil.

Place the steaks in the skillet. The cooking time totally depends on the thickness and density of the steak, but will probably be around 8 minutes per side. You should aim for medium-rare, which produces the least shrinkage, preserves moisture and still cooks the meat enough so that the texture isn't raw. The interior temperature should reach 139°F/59°C. When they get there, remove the steaks from the pan and let them rest for about 3 minutes. This will prevent all the liquid from rushing out when you cut into it.

Drop the fries into the deep fryer and cook until well browned. When they are done, drain and toss them in with the arugula. Sprinkle with salt. Spread the mixture on a heated platter.

Cut the steaks into ⅔-inch/7 mm slices. Place over the fries. Top it all with the mushroom gravy.

Serve with a steak knife and a Ballantine pounder.

POT ROAST BLEU

This is comfort food for the new millennium: familiar, yet modern. That's our style. Beef and blue cheese make a really cool combination. The salty, tangy bite of the cheese is a great complement to the richness of the beef in this dish. It's a little off center, left or right, classic but not quite. Be prepared for a long process, with quite a few steps. It's absolutely worth it.

SERVES 4 TO 5

Sea salt

Coarsely ground black pepper

3 lb/1361 g boneless beef chuck

2 cups/264 g onion, sliced

12 cloves garlic

2 cups/473 ml beef stock

8 red potatoes, boiled

Olive oil

1 cup/128 g peeled carrots, cut however

3 bay leaves

12 mushrooms

1 cup/132 g red onion, sliced

4 sprigs thyme

8 oz/227 g blue cheese crumbles

16 leaves kale, stemmed and oiled

Preheat your oven to 225°F/107°C. For this recipe you need a Dutch oven or other large, heavy pot that can go in the oven. Heat it up over medium-high heat.

Rub the meat with salt and pepper. Into the pot it goes. Brown well, turning as needed. Add the onions, stirring them into the fat that has rendered from the meat. Brown them well. This will take anywhere from 5 to 10 minutes, depending on how much surface area of the pot is available to them. The color is key; look for a good deep brown. Add the garlic and stir it around in the fat for 1 minute. Add the stock and cover.

Bring to a boil, then transfer the pan into the oven. It should simmer gently for about 2½ hours. You are looking for the thickest part of the roast to reach 210°F/98°C on a meat thermometer.

Remove from the heat and let cool to room temperature, then remove the meat from the pot and refrigerate for 3 hours, or overnight. This will firm up the meat to make cutting easier. Once it's cold, portion it into 7- or 8-ounce/198 to 226 g chunks. Each will be roughly fist-size. If there are scraps, they make great burritos or sandwiches.

Crank the oven to 500°F/260°C. In a blender (or with an immersion blender) puree the contents of the pot. Add stock as needed to get it moving. Once pureed, remove 1½ cups/355 ml and set it aside. Pour the rest into an 8- to 9-inch/20.5 to 23 cm oven-safe casserole dish for individual servings, or 9 x 15-inch/23 x 8 cm casserole to fit all with ¾ inch/2 cm between.

Prepare the vegetables: Smack the potatoes to break the skins, then toss them in olive oil and sprinkle with salt. Oil and salt the mushrooms and toss the red onion in oil as well.

Layer the beef on top of the puree and top with the reserved puree. Put a sprig of thyme on each piece, then sprinkle the blue cheese on the beef. Arrange the carrots, bay leaves, mushrooms, red onion and spuds around the casserole dish. Roast for 30 to 45 minutes, until browned and bubbling, with a rich smell. Top with the kale to brown lightly, 5 to 8 minutes.

Remove from the oven and let it sit for a few minutes before serving.

If ever there was a zinfandel dish for me, this is it. Crusty bread, too.

CHICKEN JERRY

While I steadfastly deny that we do (con)fusion food, I guess this one breaks the classic rules. It is a delicious fried chicken with spicy Asian sauce and blue cheese. It might be easier to understand its appeal if you think of buffalo wings with their spicy sauce and blue cheese dressing, though those were nowhere near my thoughts when I conceived this one. I was just thinking about Jerry, and how good this crazy combo is.

Vegetable oil, for frying

2 (8 oz/227 g) portions of natural, organic or free-range boneless, skinless chicken breast

½ cup/63 g all-purpose flour

2 large eggs

¼ cup/60 ml milk

1 tsp/6 g salt

1 tsp/2 g coarsely ground black pepper

1 cup/100 g panko bread crumbs

1½ cups/237 g cooked Yello Rice (page 215) or other aromatic rice

6 oz/170 g crumbled blue cheese

¾ cup/177 ml Thai sweet chili sauce (we use Mae Ploy brand)

½ cup/118 ml Sriracha

½ recipe The Usual Suspects (page 101)

In a deep fryer or heavy skillet, heat vegetable oil to 350°F/177°C. If you're using a skillet, the oil should be deep enough to immerse your chicken breasts halfway.

Put the flour in a wide bowl. Beat the eggs with the milk in a second wide bowl, and the salt, pepper and panko in a third wide bowl. Line them up. Dredge the chicken in the flour, shaking off the excess. Dip it in the egg wash, then dredge in the panko. Go back for another dip in the egg and another in the panko.

Fry in the oil, turning as needed until dark golden. Time here depends on a few variables. The magic of frying is that as long as the oil is consistently in the 350°F/177°C to 375°F/191°C range, the food is done when it is brown. Magic. (But it will probably take at least 6 minutes per side, FYI.)

I prefer a very warm 12-inch/30 cm plate for each serving. This one deserves a dramatic presentation! Place the rice in a tight pile, resembling an upside-down coffee cup. Sprinkle on the blue cheese; it's OK if some rolls off. Put the yard bird (Charlie Parker reference) on top of all, then pour on the sweet chili. Drizzle the Sriracha over the plate and the chicken. This is easy if you just squirt it from the bottle; act like the dudes on TV and stripe the heck out of the plate, getting a decent amount on the chicken. Top with The Usual Suspects.

Jerry would have this with a Singha brewski.

CHEF'S TIP: It's important to use jasmine rice or another aromatic one, like basmati, in this recipe. It's so weird it needs that exotic note. For (your favorite deity)'s sake, do not use boil-in-a-bag rice. It will not be a success, no matter what the label says.

PASTA CHICKEN

This crispy, spicy, cheesy, tomatoey fried chicken is a favorite of my son, Evan, and will probably please your kids, too (if you go easy on the red pepper). The pasta is panfried until crispy, a genius idea that I must credit to Tony, Miranda chef emeritus. If you have leftover cooked pasta, this is one of the best things you can do with it.

SERVES 1

---

1 cup/85 g dried rigatoni pasta

Extra-virgin olive oil

¼ cup/30 g semolina flour

Salt

Coarsely ground black pepper

1 (6 to 8 oz/170 to 227 g) boneless, skinless natural or organic chicken breast

½ cup/15 g leaf spinach

1 clove garlic, chopped coarsely

2 sprigs oregano

¼ tsp crushed red pepper flakes

2 oz/57 g Boursin cheese

1 tbsp/11 g Romano or Parmesan cheese, grated

½ cup/118 ml Marinated Tomato (page 217)

Cook the rigatoni for half the time the package calls for. Allow it to cool and toss it in olive oil. This is best done hours, even days, ahead.

Put the semolina flour with pinches of salt and pepper in a bowl. Dredge the breast, coating well.

Place olive oil in a skillet just big enough to hold the breast over medium heat. The oil should be deep enough to come halfway up the side of the chicken. Add the chicken and sauté until golden on both sides, about 6 minutes per side. Reserve in a warm place.

If you can multitask, while the chix is a-cookin', put a generous tablespoon/15 ml of olive oil in a 12-inch/30 cm stainless-steel or nonstick sauté pan over medium heat. Add the cooked rigatoni and let it brown and crisp, turning and flipping as needed. When more or less evenly browned (5 to 8 minutes), toss in the spinach, garlic, oregano and pepper flakes. Toss and add both cheeses. Mix coarsely. This should not be homogenous; make it "country style."

The spinach should be wilted, the pasta clumpy, everything smelling great. Turn out the pasta onto a plate. Top with the fried chicken. Put the Marinated Tomato on the side. Drizzle yet more olive oil on it for that fruity fresh flavor, and then grind some pepper. Eat.

CHICKEN X

This is a time-tested favorite. It uses components that can be made ahead—Salsa Evelyn, Black Bean Ragout, The Usual Suspects, Marinated Tomatoes—and comes together quickly, making it great for dinner parties.

The chicken is poached in a stew of salsa, tomatoes, peppers and onion, so it absorbs all of that wonderful flavor as it cooks. The great thing about poaching a chicken breast is that the process is so gentle to the bird. It doesn't force out the liquid; there's no drying out. Just juicy meat and lots of flavor.

SERVES 2

¼ cup/60 ml vegetable oil

¼ cup/30 g poblano peppers, seeded and torn into coarse pieces

¼ cup/33 g red onion, sliced

2 (8 oz/227 g) portions of boneless, skinless chicken breast

1¼ cups/296 ml Salsa Evelyn (page 224) or your favorite salsa

¾ cup/142 g Marinated Tomato (page 217)

1 cup/237 ml Black Bean Ragout (page 212)

1 cup/158 g cooked Yello Rice (page 215) or white rice

2 (10"/25 cm) flour tortillas

½ recipe The Usual Suspects (page 101)

6 tbsp/89 ml sour cream

Heat the oil in an 8- to 10-inch/20.5 to 25.5 cm skillet over medium heat. Add the poblanos and onion. Sauté to sweat the onion, about 8 minutes. When the onion is soft, transparent and sweet, add the chicken, then the salsa and tomato. Lower the heat to keep everything at a low simmer and cover. Poach for about 10 minutes.

Warm up your beans and rice. Microwaves are made for this.

In any size skillet, preferably cast iron, with no oil, over medium-high heat, toast the tortillas, without overlapping them, until slightly crispy and browned, even a little charred.

Place each tortilla in a big bowl, not quite in the middle, so some of it will go up the side of the bowl and won't get covered up. Place the chicken on top of the tortillas and cover with the sauce. Surround the chicken with piles of black beans and rice. Top it with The Usual Suspects, and serve sour cream on the side.

SWAMP CHOP

One day, while working on this very book, I raided my fridge and larder for supper. I found some parcooked risotto, a jar of Beth's Farm Market pickled hot peppers (it says "VERY HOT" right on it), some frozen okra, a center-cut pork chop and some tomatoes. There are no leftovers, only ingredients! This meal turned out to be a keeper. A kicky tomato-pepper sauce flavors the meat and the okra risotto isn't as strange as it sounds. Think of it as a deconstructed gumbo.

SERVES 1

---

1 (8 oz/227 g) center-cut boneless pork chop

Salt

Coarsely ground black pepper

3 tbsp/26 g pickled hot pepper, cut into medium dice

1 medium tomato, chopped large and salted

½ tsp dried oregano, or the leaves from 2 sprigs

Olive oil

¾ cup/138 g frozen okra, thawed and sliced

½ cup/85 g parcooked Risotto (page 109)

Heat your 9-inch/23 cm cast-iron skillet over medium-high heat. Sprinkle the chop with salt and pepper.

Place in the skillet on its fat side, so it is standing up. Hold with your tongs until it sticks to the pan. Lower the heat to medium-high. Turn the chop onto the flesh side. Cook, turning once, to medium-rare.

Meanwhile, toss the hot pepper, tomato, oregano and 2 tablespoons/30 ml of olive oil in a bowl.

Place the okra and risotto in a small saucepan over medium heat. Warm the mixture, stirring gently, and adding water until the risotto is creamy and hot.

How is that chop doing?

When both the rice and chop are done, pile the rice on a platter. Squish the chop down on one side. Surround it all with the tomato mixture. Give it all an olive oil drizzle.

ROAST CHOPS WITH APPLES, SPUDS AND CIDER

This is comfort food if there ever was some. This dish exists because of our friends at Sewall Orchard in Lincolnville. Mia and Bob run the oldest certified-organic orchard in the state. They produce the finest apples, heirloom and other varieties, and the season when we can get them is short. On a beautiful fall day, we put on our leather jackets and drove out in the Alfa Romeo Spider with the top down, windows up, heat on. Fall colors, great roads, great sports car. Maine. How lucky are we? I bought a boatload of apples, and came up with this way to use them. Apples are always great with pork, so I doubled down with cider and cider vinegar. Mashed potatoes and kale round out a perfect fall dish.

SERVES 2

---

2 (8 oz/227 g) center-cut boneless pork chops

1½ cups/363 g mashed potato

2 apples, halved and cored

More olive oil on hand (as always)

6 leaves kale (it's fall, remember?), coated in olive oil

¾ cup/177 ml cider

Drizzle cider vinegar (Sewall's is great stuff)

Salt

Coarsely ground black pepper

Preheat your oven to 375°F/191°C. On the stovetop, heat a 9-inch/23 cm heavy skillet, preferably cast iron, over medium-high heat. Place the chops fat-side down. I hope you have an exhaust fan. Brown the fat until dark, almost black, about 5 minutes.

Turn to the flat side and brown. You do not want to cook it through at this point, so don't turn to the other side.

In a 9 x 12-inch/23 x 30 cm oven-safe casserole dish, place the mashers in a pile. Next to them place the apples, cut side up. Brush both with olive oil. Add the seared chops next to them.

Into the *forno*! Bake for 10 to 20 minutes. The apples will puff up and eventually get to the consistency of applesauce. As you see the apples beginning to puff (it will be at least 10 minutes), top the entire dish with the kale leaves and roast away.

When the kale is dark green and beginning to crisp at the edges, pour in the cider. Bubble and boil it will. When everything is hot and the chops are medium or medium-rare (12 minutes or so), remove from the oven and plate. Drizzle some cider vinegar over. Finish the dish with a sprinkle of salt and pepper.

Serve with beer: a Sebago Frye's Leap, a hoppy IPA. Friends, sunset (yes, at four p.m.); all is good in this world.

GRITS WITH CHOURIÇO AND SHRIMP

This casual, homey dish packs a wallop. The comforting texture of grits gets a wakeup from spicy chouriço and peppers. It will warm your cockles, whatever a cockle is. (I hope it's appropriate for this book.)

SERVES 2 AS A MAIN COURSE OR 4 AS A STARTER

Olive oil

4 oz/113 g chouriço, diced medium

¼ cup/30 g poblano pepper, seeded and ripped in 1½"/4 cm chunks

1 jalapeño pepper, seeded and diced small

2 tbsp/17 g red onion, sliced

¼ cup/36 g fresh corn kernels, cut from the cob

Leaves from 2 sprigs oregano

1 cup/156 g stone-ground grits

3 cups/946 ml water

2 tbsp/28 g butter

Salt

1½ lb/680 g Maine shrimp, deheaded, in the shell

Place a 4-quart/4 L heavy-bottomed, nonreactive saucepan over medium heat. Pour in ¼ inch/6 mm of oil. When it's hot, add the chouriço. Brown lightly, then add the onion and peppers. Sauté until the vegetables are lightly browned, 5 minutes. Add the corn and cook for another minute, then in goes the oregano. Remove from the pan and set aside.

In the now-empty pan, put the grits, water and butter, with a pinch of salt. Increase heat to high and bring to a boil, then turn it down to medium-low for a simmer. Stir, a lot. Follow the package directions for the cooking time.

When the grits are close to done, put a medium skillet with ⅛ inch/3 mm of oil over high heat. When the oil is hot, add the shrimp, distribute them evenly and leave them alone. Stir the grits. It will take about 5 minutes for the shrimp to cook through. You're looking for shells that are browned, not burned, and a delicious smell. When done, pile the shrimp on a warm platter.

When the grits are done they will be a creamy mush, not a granular one. Stir in the sausage and vegetables. Pile the grits next to the shrimp.

Get out the napkins; it's eating time. A Schlitz pounder is the swill apropos.

CHEF'S TIP: The recipe calls for chouriço, which is a cured Portuguese sausage. The crumbly Mexican chorizo won't work as well. It also calls for Maine shrimp, which isn't always available. Fresh Carolina shrimp in the shell will be fine.

COVER GIRL

We used to call this "Balsamic Seared Natural Bone-in Pork Loin Chop with Roasted Broccoli, Caramelized Onion, Garlic, Jus and Pappardelle." Then one day there was the same thing, more or less, on the cover of a national food publication. On the cover! We changed the name.

What made seeing Cover Girl on a cover so surprising is that broccoli isn't often recognized for the sophisticated, even elegant vegetable it can be. Roasting deepens and sweetens the flavor, and creates a delightful variety of textures, from toothsome to crisp. It's a fantastic complement to a pork chop, and the soft fresh noodles bring it all together.

SERVES 2

---

2 cups/236 ml beef stock

2 (12 oz/340 g) bone-in pork loin chops (not the porterhouse cut)

¼ cup/60 ml cheap balsamic vinegar

10 oz/283 g Fresh Pasta (page 64), cut into random pieces

3 cups/273 g broccoli florets, tossed with a little olive oil

⅔ cup/88 g red onion, sliced

1 tbsp/9 g garlic, minced

Sea salt

Coarsely ground black pepper

Olive oil

Preheat your oven as high as it will go. Boil a pot of salted water for the pasta.

Place the stock in a small saucepan and boil over medium-high heat until it has reduced to ⅔ cups/158 ml.

Place the chops in a flat-bottomed dish. Add the balsamic, turning to coat.

Heat a 12-inch/30 cm cast-iron skillet over high heat. Get your tongs ready. Once you start there will be a lot going on, so take it easy on the beverages.

Cook the pasta according to the pasta recipe directions. When done, drain it over a pot. Set the pasta aside and return the water to the stove. Keep it simmering.

Spread the broccoli and onion on a sheet pan in one layer, without crowding. The broccoli needs to have lots of surface area exposed to the heat. Roast in the oven for up to half an hour. You are looking for both the onion and broccoli to be browned and tender.

Salt and pepper the chops. Place them into the skillet on their fat side, so they are standing up. Hold with your tongs until they stick to the pan. This will crisp and render the fat (pork rinds: yummy). Lower the heat to medium-high. Turn the chops onto the flesh side. We are aiming at the high side of medium-rare or the low side of medium. That is to say, pink (a favorite color of mine). Cooking evenly on a lower heat is crucial with bone-in meats, as that bone is a heat sink. It takes time to get the heat all through the meat. So go low and slow, with just enough heat to brown. Cook, turning just once, then leave it alone. It should take 10 minutes in total.

Meanwhile, check the broccoli. When done, remove it from the oven, add the garlic, mix it around and bit and let it cool.

Ready a heated platter!

Refresh the pasta in the simmering water, then drain again and toss with olive oil. Place the pasta on the platter. Top with the broccoli. Chops next. Drizzle the stock over the chops. Finish with salt and pepper.

INTERGALACTIC PORK

Being a modest guy, I used to call this Interplanetary Pork. An eater corrected me, saying, "It's not out of this world. It's out of this galaxy." I am pretty sure it was a compliment. This preparation of pork in a Thai-style curry sauce was a surprise for our diners back in the day, in a couple of ways. One is that I do not cook my pork chops until they are gray and dry. This makes people nervous; they see pink (the right color) and they think the pork is underdone. I take my customers' concerns seriously, of course, but I am not going to overcook pork chops. So I turn down the lights and everyone wins.

SERVES 2

2 center-cut boneless pork loin chops

2 tsp/10 g sesame seeds, preferably toasted, or peanuts

5 to 6 sprigs cilantro

¼ cup/25 g mung bean sprouts

2 scallions, cut diagonally into thin slices

2 lime quarters

Thai fish sauce

1 cup/237 ml vegetable oil

1 sweet potato, cut into matchsticks (as close as you can to French fries)

¼ red onion, sliced

2 tbsp/50 g red curry paste

½ cup/118 ml coconut milk

½ cup/113 g fresh corn kernels, cut from the cob (or frozen)

1 cup/30 g baby spinach

5 leaves basil

If brining is your thing, brine the chops. We use leftover pickle juice and let them sit an hour or two. You can skip this.

Heat a 9-inch/23 cm pan over medium-high heat. Put the chops fat-side down. Count to 60, then flip onto the flat side. Watch the side of the chops. When the bottom third is gray, flip it and repeat so that the top and bottom thirds are both gray. Remove from the pan and keep covered in a warm place.

In a bowl, place the sesame seeds, cilantro, bean sprouts and scallions. Squeeze the lime over and sprinkle with fish sauce.

Place ½ inch/1.5 cm of oil in a 12-inch/30 cm skillet over medium heat. Heat until it sizzles if you spit in it (only do this at home, folks). Add the sweet potato and sauté until tender and starting to brown. Carefully pour off most of the oil.

Turn up the heat to high. This is now a stir-fry. Add the onion and push everything to one side of the pan. Put in the curry paste and fry for a few seconds, until fragrant but not brown. Put in the coconut milk and corn and stir together with the curry; keep the vegetables on the side. When blended, add the spinach, basil and sweet potato fries. Then stir everything together.

Put on a plate, add the pork chops and put the bean sprout mixture on top.

THE HEADACRE

This is another one of those dinners that emerged from the fridge, larder and garden at Headacre Farm. It's a pork chop over grits with peppers, onions and tomatoes. Can't go wrong there. What makes it really special is the basil salad: all the varieties you can pull from your garden, piled on top of it all. Thanks to Farmer Anne I had five varieties to work with, but even if you just have one, you'll find that a basil salad is a perfect contrast to hearty, substantial fare.

SERVES 2

4 small Italian frying peppers

Extra-virgin olive oil (Just have a lot around, OK?)

Salt

2 ripe tomatoes

2 cipollini onions

2 (8 oz/227 g) boneless pork chops

Coarsely ground black pepper

2 cups/60 g mixed basil leaves

2 cloves garlic, minced

2 tbsp/30 ml balsamic vinegar

1 cup/237 g cooked grits (I use an organic brand from below the Mason-Dixon Line, even farther south than Kittery)

Get a 10-inch/25.5 cm (or larger) cast-iron pan on medium heat. Warm your oven with a platter inside.

Wash your peppers, rub them with oil and sprinkle with salt. Cut the tomatoes into largish chunks, and salt them. Peel the onions and halve them crosswise, so you see the rings as you would on a log. If you cut logs, that is. I do.

Place the onions in the hot pan. No oil! This will smoke in 2 minutes, more or less. Turn. Cook through, about 4 minutes per side, turning as needed to keep one side from charring too much. When cooked through, place on the platter in the oven.

Cook the tomatoes as you did the onion, about 7 minutes on each side. You want a char on the outside, hot on the inside. If you cook them too long, they turn to delicious mush. No fear, it'll work. Add to the platter.

It's the peppers' turn in the pan. You want to turn them often; if you overdo the skin, it will be brittle and bitter. Once they are heated through and browned on the inside, you're done. It will take 8 minutes or so. Transfer to the platter.

Turn up the heat under the pan to medium-high.

Season the chops with salt and pepper. Place in the pan fat-side down. Yes, this means they are standing on their side. The idea is to accelerate the rendering of fat and making of browned goodness. Keep them there for around 5 minutes, then lay them down in the pan on the broad side. Cook to medium-rare. They will be pinkish inside and a meat thermometer will give you 140°F/60°C.

Meanwhile, toss the basil leaves with the garlic, balsamic and some olive oil. Use enough oil to coat well, then add another couple of tablespoons.

When the chops are done, place them on the platter. Top with the basil salad. Serve with the grits.

PORK MOLE

This has little to do with traditional mole. Sue me. It is a fantastic way to eat pork, with the deep spice of Sauce El Camino perked up by fried banana and a hit of cocoa. Serve it with The Usual Suspects for a fresh accent and a hot, Caribbean-style mustard.

SERVES 2

---

2 (8 oz/227 g) center-cut pork chops

1 not-quite-ripe banana, peeled, cut on the bias into 1"/2.5 cm slices

¾ cup/177 ml Sauce El Camino (page 216), hot

4 oz/113 g Mexican chocolate, or 2 tbsp/11 g unsweetened cocoa powder

⅔ cup/151 g Black Bean Ragout (page 212), hot

2 tbsp/30 ml Caribbean-style mustard

⅔ cup/58 g The Usual Suspects (page 101)

Put a 9-inch/23 cm cast-iron skillet over high heat. Preheat your oven to 300°F/149°C.

Sear the chop. First stand it on the fatty edge for about 5 minutes, holding it with tongs until it will stand alone. This will render and crisp the fat. When most of the fat is gone, lay it down, searing the sides while leaving the inside still rare and cool. This will take about 3 minutes on each side. After searing, pop the chops in the oven to slow-roast for about 10 minutes. Take them to a thermometer reading of 138°F/59°C in the center of the thickest part.

In another 9-inch/23 cm skillet, place enough oil to come up ½ inch/1.5 cm. Heat it to 350°F to 375°F/177°C to 191°C. Fry the banana until golden brown, 5 to 7 minutes, turning once. Drain on a rack.

Whisk the chocolate into the hot El Camino. Pour the sauce onto one side of a heated platter. Put the ragout on the other side, and the banana on another one. The chops go in the middle. Squirt mustard over it all. Put The Usual Suspects on top of the chops and serve.

SCALOPPINE OF PORK MILANESE

Listen to this: Romano-breaded, panfried scaloppine of pork tenderloin with warm tomato coulis, served with roasted broccoli rabe. Is there anyone (OK, the vegetarians) who wouldn't swoon over this classy dish? It is so simple and delicious, right to the point. There's no need to serve it with a starch; the breading takes care of it.

This requires some help from your butcher. Ask him or her to clean and pound (like veal) 4-ounce/113 g pieces of the tenderloin to about 1/3 inch/3.5 mm thick.

SERVES 1

COULIS

1 ripe tomato, diced

Leaves from a sprig oregano

2 cloves garlic, peeled

3 tbsp/45 ml good olive oil

Salt

Coarsely ground black pepper

1 large egg

2 tbsp/30 ml heavy cream

1/3 cup/40 g unseasoned bread crumbs

1/4 cup/44 g Romano cheese, grated finely

All-purpose flour

2 (4 oz/113 g) scaloppine of pork tenderloin, pounded

1/4 cup/60 ml decent olive oil, for frying

1/4 cup/57 g clarified butter

1/4 cup/33 g red onion, sliced

4 stalks broccoli rabe, tough ends cut off (about 2"/5 cm from the bottom)

Olive oil, yes, more

Salt

Coarsely ground black pepper

Preheat your oven to 400°F/204°C.

Make the coulis: Drop the tomato, oregano, garlic and good olive oil into your blender. Blend until smooth and add salt and pepper to taste. Transfer into a microwave-safe measuring cup (or another vessel that's easy to pour from) and microwave until warm, not hot.

Now to bread the porkee. Put the flour in a bowl. In another bowl, beat the egg with the cream. In another bowl, mix the bread crumbs with the Romano. Drag the pork through the flour for just a bare coating, which will help the egg wash stick. Dip the pork in the egg wash and let it drip off. Place it into the crumb mixture. Gently press the bread crumb mixture into the pork. Transfer to a plate.

Heat the olive oil and clarified butter in a 12-inch/30 cm stainless-steel skillet over medium-high heat to 350°F/177°C, or until a drop of water will sizzle. It's crucial that the oil be hot enough. If, when you add the pork, you don't see any visible frying action, get the pork out of there! Heat the oil some more and then try again.

Cook the pork to a golden brown, turning once, 5 to 6 minutes per side. Drain on paper towels.

Whilst this is going on (did I say this was simple?), toss the onion and rabe in some oil, place on a cookie sheet and roast for about 8 minutes. Sprinkle with salt and pepper.

We now have warm coulis, fried pork, roasted rabe.

On a big, warm plate put 2 dabs (American dabs, not metric) of the coulis, where the pork will go. This will keep it from sticking to the plate. Put the pork on each dab. Drizzle the rest of the coulis, Pollack style, around the meat and the plate. Don't cover the pork, though. Arrange the rabe stuff around the border.

PITCH A TENT

This is stick-to-your-ribs comfort food for a winter's day. Delicious roasted sausage, pasta and kale in a brown cream sauce will warm you right up. But the best part is setting it down in front of someone and seeing them put two and two together.

SERVES 2

---

4 (4 oz/115 g) sausage links (Pearl brand knockwurst preferred; sweet Italian sausage is good, too)

2 tbsp/30 ml olive oil, plus more for brushing

1 red onion, sliced

8 cloves garlic

¼ cup/59 ml fortified wine

½ cup/118 ml heavy cream

1 cup/237 ml brown beef stock (homemade or lower-sodium canned)

2 (6" x 6"/15 x 15 cm) sheets of Fresh Pasta (page 64) or fresh lasagna sheets

8 leaves kale, stemmed and ripped up, tossed in olive oil

Put on a pot of water to boil for the pasta. Preheat your oven to 350°F/177°C.

Brush the sausages with oil (the fun starts here) and place in a 9-inch/23 cm oven-safe casserole dish. Place in the oven and cook, turning a few times, until well browned, 10 to 15 minutes. Don't boil them first—you want to keep the fat in the dish. If you're using knockwurst, they are already cooked, so just get them brown and hot.

Heat the 2 tablespoons/30 ml of olive oil in a 12-inch/30 cm skillet over medium heat. Add the onion and garlic and cook until the onion caramelizes, 8 minutes. When it is very soft and light brown, pour in the fortified wine and stir to deglaze the pan. Add the cream and beef stock.

Cook the sauce for about 6 minutes, until it has reduced and thickened enough to coat a spoon (if you pick it up, it won't drip and hit your tie). Set aside.

Cook the pasta according to the pasta recipe or package directions. Set aside.

When the sausages have browned, add the kale and stir it around in the fat so that it fries in the pan. It will take about 6 minutes to cook through. When the color has intensified and the edges are crisp, take out the kale.

Add the sauce to the casserole dish (if it's a glass casserole, make sure the pan and sauce are close to the same temperature). If the sauce has gotten too thick, add water or stock. Put the casserole back in the oven to warm.

On a serving platter, spread half the sauce and all the kale. Put down the sausages in two crossed pairs and place a sheet of pasta over each pair. Pour the remaining sauce liberally over all. Snicker. Then eat.

SMOKED MEAT LOAF

You don't have a smoker? Do not fret! We can do it in your oven. Smoking your meat loaf has several advantages. First, it will answer the question your friends have been asking for years, about what you have been smoking. Now you can say, "Meat loaf. You?" Second, it sets you up for the best NASCAR Pâté (page 194). Third, smoked meat loaf just beats the pants off regular meat loaf. If you can't imagine why, you need more smoked food in your life.

SERVES 3 TO 4

½ cup/66 g celery, minced

3 tbsp/27 g garlic, minced

1¼ cups/165 g onion, minced

1½ tsp/2.5 g coriander seeds

2 bay leaves

3 tbsp/45 ml olive oil, plus more for brushing

½ lb/227 g ground pork

½ lb/227 g ground veal

2 large eggs

⅓ cup/40 g unseasoned bread crumbs

1 tsp salt

1 leaf sage, minced

2½ tsp/6 g coarsely ground black pepper

½ cup/120 ml quality barbecue sauce

In a large, heavy skillet over medium heat, sweat the celery, garlic and onion with the coriander seeds, bay leaves and olive oil. Cook the mixture until the onion is opaque, 15 minutes at least. Chill the mixture thoroughly.

In a larger bowl or a stand mixer with the paddle attachment, place all the remaining ingredients, except the barbecue sauce, and mix well.

Brush a 6 x 10-inch/15 x 25.5 cm loaf pan with olive oil and fill with the mixture. Top with the barbecue sauce.

If you have a smoker, get it going. If not, preheat your oven to 300°F/149°C. Place 1 cup of soaked and drained wood chips (maple, apple or hickory) in a cast-iron skillet on the range top on high heat. They gotta smoke. Have your exhaust fan on! When they are good and smoky, put the pan on the bottom rack of the oven. Put the loaf on the middle rack and bake them happily together for about 80 minutes. The center of the loaf should come up to a temperature of at least 155°F/68°C. Let cool on a rack in the pan, then chill.

Meat loaf is better the next day, and is also easier to get out of the pan and slice. Dip the pan into warm water and run a knife around the side. Put a plate on top, invert and remove the pan. Wa-la!

POLENTA PIZZA CASSEROLE

One of my friends has semi-fond memories of childhood days when her father, left responsible for a meal, would make "pizza casserole." It was a combination of whatever canned things were in the cupboards, doused in cheese and baked for a bit. The magic came from the name: Kids will eat a pizza casserole.

The name is the only thing that's similar about this one. The flavors of pizza are brought to their comfort-food apotheosis when firm polenta is layered with marinara, cheese and mushrooms, and it all bakes together into a gooey, warm, totally fulfilling dish for a winter evening. Calling it pizza casserole won't hurt, though, if you're trying to get kids to eat.

SERVES 2

4 (4" x 4"/10 x 10 cm) squares of firm Polenta (page 108)

12 medium button mushrooms

Olive oil (Just have some around; it seems to be in everything)

1½ cups/356 ml Latex Marinara (page 218)

6 oz/170 g ricotta cheese

2 tbsp/22 g Romano or Parmesan cheese, grated

8 leaves basil

¾ cup/100 g mozzarella cheese, shredded

Preheat your oven to 375°F/191°C.

Cut the polenta squares diagonally to make 8 triangles. Cut the mushrooms in half and coat them with olive oil.

In a shallow, 9 x 12-inch/23 x 30 cm oven-safe casserole dish, place the marinara, reserving ¼ cup/60 ml for later. Stand the triangles in the casserole, pointing up. Divide the ricotta and Romano between each wedge. Top the cheese with a basil leaf. Sprinkle the mozzarella over everything.

Stripe the remaining marinara down the middle, to give it a good "face." Place the mushrooms around the perimeter.

Into the oven! Bake until dark golden brown and bubbly, 45 minutes or more. Caution: Do not burn your upper mouth! That "pizza burn" is awful.

MEAT LOAF AND POTATOES DINNER

This is a perfect way to serve Smoked Meat Loaf (page 132): roasted with potatoes, green beans and lots of flavorful sauce.

Slice your meat loaf thickly, in 2½- to 3-inch/6 to 8 cm slices. Thin slices will dry out during the roasting.

SERVES 1

3 red potatoes, boiled
Olive oil
Salt
Coarsely ground black pepper
⅛ cup/17 g red onion, sliced
1 thick slice of Smoked Meat Loaf (page 132)
¼ cup/60 ml Salsa Evelyn (page 224)
12 green beans, ends snipped
2 tbsp/30 ml barbecue sauce
6 tbsp/90 ml beef stock
1½ tbsp/22 ml Caribbean-style mustard

Preheat your oven to 400°F/204°C. Use an 8-inch/20 cm oven-safe casserole dish for a single serving. Place the potatoes in one side and smack them to break the skins. Brush with oil and sprinkle with salt and pepper. Take half of the onion and put it on the bottom in roughly the shape of the meat loaf slice. This will insulate the meat from the pan, keeping it from drying out. Put the meat loaf slice on top of the onion.

In a bowl, toss together the salsa, green beans and the remaining onion along with a bit of oil. Place aside the other stuff in the casserole. Top the loaf with the barbecue sauce. Bake.

Around 18 minutes into baking, add the stock. This will pick up all the present flavors and make a fine pan sauce, with no work from you. After another 7 minutes or so, you should see that the loaf is heated through, the beans are done but still fresh-colored, the spuds browning and the sauce has a fine brown glaze. Remove from the oven.

Dollop the mustard on the meat and serve with beer. An American classic like a Schlitz is apropos for the loaf.

PIEROGIES À LA PINK PLATE

Some of my earliest memories are of eating boiled 'rogies with sautéed onions and butter, or deep-fried ones with sour cream. This version puts the Polish ravioli in its natural environment, with cabbage, onion and mushrooms. It's a simple, throw-together weeknight meal that your kids and grandkids might be remembering fondly decades hence. I first made this version in 1993 and served it on pink plates that were antique even then. They have ever since been the pink-plate pierogies.

SERVES 1

6 tbsp/90 ml olive oil

½ cup/66 g onion, diced medium

¾ cup/50 g button mushrooms, smashed

3 cloves garlic, minced

1½ cups/134 g green cabbage, chopped

4 frozen potato and cheese pierogies, thawed

¼ cup/60 ml balsamic vinegar

3 tbsp/43 g butter

¼ cup/20 g fresh parsley

Salt

Coarsely ground black pepper

Use a large nonstick skillet. Put it over high heat. Heat the oil. When it's rippling, gently add the onion and stir. Be careful of splatters.

When the onion begins to brown, after about 5 minutes, add the mushrooms and stir. Cook for another 5 minutes or so. Add the garlic and stir. Wow, what an aroma! As the garlic toasts and begins to change color, add the cabbage and stir. Keep cooking on high heat, as you want to brown the cabbage. Keep stirring occasionally. When all this cabbage and such first goes in the pan, it is a huge volume. The volume of the veg will reduce as the cells break down, the liquid evaporates and things caramelize. This will take a while, 10 to 15 minutes. Patience, sailor.

When the cabbage is tender and browned, add the pierogies and stir carefully. Don't break the 'rogies! Heat through, about 5 minutes. When they are heated and the vegetable matter is beautiful and browned, add the balsamic. Again, watch out for the spatter. Let the vinegar evaporate and reduce a bit, intensifying the flavors.

Remove from the heat and stir in the butter. This will bind the various liquids to a sauce.

Technique note: The method of emulsifying a sauce by whisking in cold butter is called mounting, and you'll find it in all kinds of fancy French sauces like beurre blanc. It works just as well for the humble pieróg.

Throw in the Elvis Parsley, salt and pepper, and toss the whole shebang. Plate on a large platter, preferably pink.

CHEF'S TIP: We don't make our own pierogies. The Mrs. T's brand is made by a family I grew up with in the coal country of Pennsylvania, and I am proud to use this fine (and cheap) product. You can use whatever brand you prefer.

EGGPLANT PARMESAN

This is soul food for Italian Americans: a supple, rich, creamy Eggplant Parmesan that takes much less time and effort than the traditional preparation. Most recipes call for salting the eggplant to get rid of bitter juices, then dipping in flour, egg wash, bread crumbs, and so on. Here olive oil and a hot oven fry/roast out the bitterness without much effort from you at all. You can even skip peeling the eggplant; if you don't peel them, the slices will be easier to handle after cooking.

SERVES 2

1 large eggplant (1 lb/454 g or more)

Olive oil

Salt

Coarsely ground black pepper

1½ cups/356 ml Latex Marinara (page 218)

4 leaves basil

5 oz/142 g whole-milk mozzarella cheese, shredded

2 oz/57 g Parmesan or Romano, grated

½ lb/227 g dried rigatoni pasta

¼ cup/20 g fresh parsley, chopped

1 tsp red pepper flakes

1 cup/30 g spinach, stemmed and tossed in olive oil

Preheat your oven to 425°F/218°C.

Trim the top and bottom of your eggplant to give you flat surfaces, then slice into 2½-inch/6 cm slices. Trust me—you want them thick.

Ready a cookie sheet that will hold the slices without overlapping.

Put ½ cup/120 ml or so of olive oil into a medium bowl. Put the cookie sheet next to the bowl. Mess alert: This is gonna be drippy. Dip a slice of the eggplant in the oil, then turn it over and let it swim for a minute. You'll see the color change a bit, the way a sponge does when it soaks up liquid, which is exactly what is happening. Lift out of the oil and let the excess drain off, then put the slice back on the sheet. Repeat with the rest of the eggplant. Sprinkle the slices with salt and pepper.

Into the oven! This part requires some vigilance. It will start slowly but accelerate. Check after 15 minutes; it will probably take 25. The eggplant should be browned, not burned, cooked through, quite soft. Pierce it with a skewer. If it passes through easily and consistently, it's done. If the eggplant browns too quickly, cover it with foil.

When done, let cool. You can store for 2 or 3 days at this point.

Boil a pot of water for the pasta.

Take 2 (8-inch/20 cm) oven-safe casserole dishes. Cover the bottom of each with the marinara. Distribute the eggplant over it, and put the basil on top. Cover with the cheeses. This will protect the eggplant from additional charring. Return to the oven and bake until crusty, brown, and bubbling, about 12 minutes.

When you see the first signs of browning, drop your pasta in the water and cook to al dente. Drain, then toss with parsley, 1 tablespoon (15 ml) olive oil, salt, pepper and red pepper flakes.

At the last minute, put the spinach on top of the casseroles. Let it wilt and get a little brown. Carefully remove from the oven. Place each on an underliner plate and surround with the pasta.

This totally calls for wine in a basket, crusty bread, a checked tablecloth, maybe a black light and some gondolas painted on the walls.

THE WOWIES: LAMB OR VEG

These are my take on some sort of a pan-Indian-Whateverstan stew with condiments. The flavor is similar to a curry but more savory, without the perfumy elements of cinnamon and such that curries often have. The name was the first thing out of my mouth when I tried it for the first time.

We have a customer who lives in Boothbay Harbor, Maine, who is of South Asian heritage. When she ordered a Wowie, I cringed. While I am happy to borrow from all the great cuisines of the world, I don't make any attempts at authenticity and I don't want to be compared to anyone's grandmother. If a Korean comes in and asks to try the kimchi, I run interference: "No way. Get the spaghetti and meatballs." Anyway, our Boothbay customer got the dish after all. She came right up to the counter and said, "Who are you and how do you know how to do this?" I seem to have lucked into something authentic after all, unencumbered by actual knowledge or experience.

SERVES 4

½ cup/64 g carrot, shredded

2 tbsp/18 g raisins

½ lemon

2 tsp/9 g black sesame seeds

½ cup/66 g red onion, sliced

Coarse salt

1 cup/160 g tomato, diced

2 tbsp/30 ml Tabasco or other acidic hot sauce

½ cup/60 g cucumber, shredded or minced

1 recipe Lamb or Veg Wowie stew (recipe follows), hot

2 cups/372 g cooked Yello Rice (page 215) or other aromatic rice

1 cup/237 ml plain yogurt

Sprigs of cilantro

Prepare the condiments in little bowls: Mix the carrot and raisins and squeeze the lemon over. Add a sprinkle of black sesame seeds. In another bowl, sprinkle the onion with salt and mix. In a third, mix the tomato with the Tabasco. The cucumber goes in another bowl, with a squeeze of lemon.

In flat-bottomed, low-sided bowls, place the rice in a pile. Pour the stew next to it, keeping it mostly separate. Dollop the yogurt on top, sprinkle with some black sesame seeds and strew cilantro sprigs over it all. Serve the condiments on the side in the little bowls.

LAMB WOWIE

This makes enough for four servings. If you don't need that much, it will keep for a week in the fridge, or you can freeze it. Like all stews, ragouts or Wowies, this gets better if it sits at least overnight.

SERVES 4

¼ cup/60 ml vegetable oil

1 red onion, sliced

6 cloves garlic, peeled

2 ribs celery, chopped coarsely

½ cup/35 g carrot, minced

2 poblano peppers, seeded and chopped coarsely

2 bay leaves

1½ lb/680 g lamb, cut into 1"/2.5 cm cubes

¾ cup/177 ml canned crushed tomato

¼ cup/25 g Secret Spice (page 224)

4 cups/120 g spinach

Preheat your oven to 250°F/121°C.

Heat the oil in a 5- to 6-quart/5 to 6 L heavy, oven-safe pot over medium heat. Sauté the onion and garlic until the onion is translucent and sweet, 6 to 8 minutes. Add the celery, carrots and peppers. Partially cover and continue cooking until the vegetables are tender, but not browned, 12 minutes or so. Add the bay leaves, lamb, tomato, Secret Spice and about ½ cup/118 ml of water.

Move the pot into the oven, covered. Cook until the lamb is tender, up to 3 hours. Stir every once in a while and add more water if it seems to be needed. Remove from the oven and add in spinach to wilt. Then serve as described on page 139, or let cool and refrigerate until ready to use.

VEG WOWIE I

Follow recipe for Lamb Wowie, replacing the meat with 1½ pounds/680 g of cauliflower, cut into large pieces. Be very sparing of your stirring while it is in the oven, as too much will result in mushy vegetables. The cooking time will be much less, an hour at most.

VEG WOWIE II

¾ cup/177 ml coconut milk

2 tbsp/13 g Secret Spice (page 224)

2 tsp/6 g ginger, minced

2 tsp/6 g garlic, minced

15 raisins

3 oz/85 g dried sheep's milk cheese (ricotta salata, feta, or paneer)

6 cups/180 g spinach, destemmed

Heat all but the spinach to a boil. Remove from heat and add spinach. Cover until spinach wilts.

GNU THING

This is a quick, Indian-inspired, stewish entrée: tofu, potato and green beans in a coconut curry, with lentils. It is exotic, vegetarian (vegan if you omit the yogurt) and hearty enough for a chilly day while being bright enough for a hot day. We have had many "Gnu" dishes, but the name stuck on this one. It always seems new and exciting, no matter how often you've made it.

SERVES 1

¾ cup/113 g cooked Yello Rice (page 215)

6 tbsp/85 g ghee or clarified butter

4 oz/113 g tofu, cut into 1"/2.5 cm cubes

8 green beans, ends snipped

½ cup/66 g red onion, sliced

2 red potatoes, cooked and quartered

½ cup/118 ml coconut milk

4 tsp/8 g Secret Spice (page 224)

2 tsp/6 g fresh ginger, minced

2 tsp/6 g garlic, minced

Salt

¼ cup/54 g Lentil Doll (page 214)

2 tbsp/30 ml plain yogurt

2 tbsp/15 g cucumber, seeded and shredded (or use a European cucumber)

2 lemon wedges

2 sprigs cilantro

Warm up your rice.

Heat the ghee over high heat in a 12-inch/30 cm skillet. Add the tofu and fry, stirring occasionally, to get it to golden brown, about 5 minutes. Remove the tofu from the pan and replace with the green beans. Stir-fry for about a minute, until the color brightens. They should still be crunchy. Push the beans to the side of the pan. Add the onion and potatoes. Fry for another 2 minutes, or until the potatoes are heated through. Add the coconut milk, Secret Spice, ginger and garlic. Mix it all together. Add salt to taste.

On a heated platter, mound the rice, and spoon the mixture from the pan onto it. Don't cover it all up; let some be on the side. Put the cold Doll on one side. Ditto for the yogurt. Put the cuke on the yogurt and squeeze the lemon over it all. Put the cilantro on top.

OVEN-BAKED FRITTATA

This frittata is stuffed with Cheddar, bacon, tomato and greens, and flavored with garlic and basil. It is a totally satisfying time for any meal of the day, while being quite a bit lighter than most of the entries in this chapter. Try making several and serving a crowd for brunch—it's very easy on the host. Baking a frittata in the oven removes the trouble of getting the top and bottom cooked that you deal with on the stovetop. Even better, the even heat of the oven makes the eggs especially puffy and tender.

SERVES 1

---

1 tbsp/15 g butter

1 oz/28 g uncooked bacon, chopped

2 tbsp/17 g onion, sliced

1 tsp olive oil

1 tsp garlic, minced

⅛ cup/20 g tomato, diced

1½ oz/43 g sharp Cheddar cheese, shredded

2 leaves basil

3 large eggs, beaten

½ cup/15 g spinach, stemmed and tossed in olive oil

Bread, to serve

Preheat your oven to 350°F/177°C. In an 8-inch/20 cm casserole dish, place the butter. Add the bacon and onion. Roast to lightly brown the onion and bacon, 8 to 10 minutes. Stir in the oil and garlic and let it sizzle. Add the tomato, cheese and basil. Stir in the egg and mix it all well. Top with the spinach.

Return the dish to the oven for 15 to 20 minutes. The frittata will cook from the sides toward the center, poofing up as it cooks. When you see that the center has poofed, poke the middle with a toothpick. It should come back damp, but not wet. No one likes runny eggs in a frittata.

Serve hot, or at room temperature, with bread.

HUEVOS MIRANDA

Here's another oven dish that's great for entertaining. It is highly idiot-resistant, so it works for me. This one is baked eggs, swimming in flavorful beans and sauce, to be scooped up with homemade tortilla chips. Use fresh, local eggs if you can get them. They make a big difference.

SERVES 1

6 tbsp/89 ml Black Bean Ragout (page 212), warm

2 large eggs

Olive oil

Vegetable oil, for frying

2 corn tortillas, quartered

¼ cup/60 ml Sauce El Camino (page 216), hot

¼ cup/22 g The Usual Suspects (page 101)

¼ cup/60 ml Salsa Evelyn (page 224)

Preheat your oven to 400°F/204°C.

In a small, heavy casserole dish, spread the ragout, making it a little thinner in the middle of the dish. Crack the eggs on top. Drizzle some olive oil over the eggs so that they will fry a bit. Into the oven they go.

Fry your chips: In a deep fryer or heavy skillet, get your vegetable oil hot, 350°F/177°C. Drop the tortillas into the oil, stirring as to not allow them to spoon or stick together. Cook until golden and crispy, about 5 minutes. Drain on a rack or paper towels.

Bake the eggs until the whites are just set and the yolks still liquid, around 10 minutes. Remove from the oven. Place the chips around the edges of the casserole. Be an artist. Pour the El Camino onto the chips. Put the slaw on one side of the eggs. Serve with the salsa.

SECRET SCALLOPS

The secret is our Secret Spice, which gives a warm, exotic, indefinable flavor to oven-roasted scallops. The scallops are cooked in a flavorful stew of tomato, olives, ginger and garlic, with a sprinkle of raisins for sweetness. A good serving of spinach and my favorite yellow jasmine rice rounds out the meal. This dish requires some prep, but once it goes into the oven, it will be done in 10 minutes. It's easy to scale, too, so it's a winner for dinner parties.

SERVES 1

¾ cup/142 g Marinated Tomato (page 217)

8 good green pitted olives, broken by squishing between your fingers

1 tbsp/9 g raisins or currants

1 tsp fresh ginger, minced

1 tsp garlic, minced

2 tsp/4 g Secret Spice (page 224)

6 oz/170 g dry sea scallops, sweet meats removed (see chef's tip)

Salt

Coarsely ground black pepper

1 cup/142 g cooked Yello Rice (page 215)

1½ cups/45 g spinach, stemmed and tossed in olive oil

3 leaves basil

2 tsp extra-virgin olive oil

2 tbsp/15 g cucumber, shredded

2 sprigs cilantro

Lemon wedge

1 tsp black sesame seeds

Preheat your oven to 450°F/232°C. Choose an oven-safe casserole dish that will hold the ingredients in one layer. For a single serving, you can use a 9-inch/23 cm dish.

Place the tomato, olives, raisins, ginger, garlic, olive oil and Secret Spice in the casserole.

Mix well. Add the scallops and get them well coated with the mixture. Sprinkle with salt and pepper. Put it in the oven on the middle rack.

As the stew is heating up, warm up your rice.

After 7 minutes, stir the spinach and basil into the tomato mixture. Cook for another 3 minutes or so. The spinach should wilt and provide a smooth, supple texture to the dish. Make sure everything is good and hot. The scallops don't need to be hot through (raw scallops are great!) but shouldn't be cold in the middle. The worst is for them to be overcooked; they will shrink and split. Yuck. Remove the casserole from the oven before that happens.

On the heated plate, place the rice in a tight pile. Make a well in the center. Spoon and pour the scallop mixture into the well. Top with a pile of cucumber and lay the cilantro about. Squeeze the lemon wedge. Sprinkle the black sesame seeds over all.

CHEF'S TIP: Sweet meats are a cute description of the hard piece of flesh on the side of the scallop that attaches the scallop to the shell. Tough stuff here. These can be saved and frozen and used to make a seafood stock or pureed in a mousseline.

GENTEEL HADDOCK

The name says it all here. An Atlantic haddock fillet is gently poached in buttery broth, and served with a sheet of pasta, roasted tomato, red onion and spinach. It is a refined dinner that calls for actual table manners.

You can substitute low-salt natural clam juice or even vegetable stock for the fish stock.

SERVES 2

2 (5" x 5"/13 x 13 cm) sheets of Fresh Pasta (page 64)

3 ripe Roma tomatoes, split tip to point

The requisite EVOO

Coarse sea salt

Coarsely ground black pepper

¼ cup/33 g red onion, sliced

1 tsp garlic, minced

2 cups/60 g spinach, stemmed if needed, tossed in olive oil

2 (8-oz/227 g) North Atlantic haddock fillets

1½ cups/355 ml fish stock

¼ cup/57 g unsalted butter

Preheat your oven to 400°F/204°C.

In a 4-quart/4 L saucepan, cook the sheets of pasta until al dente, 5 to 7 minutes. Remove and set aside. Return the water to the stove and turn down the heat so that it stays at a simmer.

In a 6 x 9-inch/15 x 23 cm oven-safe casserole dish, place the tomatoes, inside up. Slather them with olive oil and crust with lots of salt, then pepper. Put in the oven. After 15 minutes, add the onion and stir to coat with oil. Continue roasting until the tomatoes are cooked through, probably about half an hour. Remove from the oven. Stir in the garlic, then leave to cool for a few minutes.

Place a layer of spinach in the casserole, and place the fillets on top of that. Coat the fish with olive oil, pepper and a little salt. Add the stock.

Return the casserole to the oven. The goal is to just barely cook the fish and wilt the spinach. It will take 15 minutes or less. Cook the fish until it is done to your taste (mine is, as one staffer put it, "just done enough so they won't send it back"). A well-cooked piece of fish will be bright white on the outside. The interior will be translucent until it is cooked through. Use a fork to gently pull apart a teeny section in the thickest part of the fillet. You want it to be just barely past translucent, moving toward white. At this point, remove it from the oven and add the butter. Let it melt, stirring gently.

Put your pasta sheets back in the pan of simmering water to refresh, then drain. Toss the sheets in some olive oil. Arrange them around the fish.

White Bordeaux and a baguette make for a classic, fashionable, genteel repast.

HADDOCK ENCHILADA

This is really a kind of cousin to the enchilada. It involves tortillas, a filling and a sauce, all cooked in the oven, but it's arranged rather differently than is traditional. The combination of beans, haddock, peppers and cheese is irresistible. This makes a big serving, but if you manage to leave some on the plate, I'll be surprised.

SERVES 1

---

2 tbsp/30 ml vegetable oil

¼ cup/33 g onion, sliced

½ cup/60 g poblano pepper, seeded and ripped coarsely

½ cup/118 ml Sauce El Camino (page 216) with 2 tbsp/30 ml water mixed in

5 (6"/15 cm) corn tortillas (get the good ones)

¼ cup/56 g corn kernels (fresh ifyagotit)

4 oz/113 g fresh north Atlantic haddock

2 oz/56 g ricotta or other fresh cheese

1 oz/28 g Cheddar cheese, shredded

⅓ cup/30 g The Usual Suspects (page 101)

½ cup/106 g Black Bean Ragout (page 212)

⅓ cup/47 g cooked Yello Rice (page 215)

Preheat your oven to 375°F/191°C. In a 9-inch/23 cm oven-safe casserole dish, place the oil, onion and poblano. Roast in the oven until the onion caramelizes a bit. Say, 8 or so minutes. De-pan the vegetables and set aside.

In the casserole dish, place half of the Sauce El Camino. Lay 3 of the tortillas on the sauce. Arrange so that one is centered in the casserole, they overlap just a bit and the tortillas hang over the edge of the dish. Place the pepper mixture, corn and haddock on the tortillas. Fold them over the mixture and top with the remaining 2 tortillas. Pour the remaining sauce over, place a scoop of fresh cheese on top and sprinkle with the Cheddar

Return to the oven and bake until bubbling and heated through, about 45 minutes. Remove and top with the Usual Suspects, with the ragout and rice on the side. Serve in the casserole dish.

Oh, a Tecate with a lime and salt is just the ticket!

OVEN-ROASTED FISH TACOS

These are a lunchtime favorite at the restaurant. Eating them does call for a lot of napkins, but this is still a great group snack. You can prep all the ingredients and let all of your friends/guests/enemies get silly building tacos. Fun!

SERVES 2

8 (6"/15 cm) corn tortillas (try to get the thicker artisanal type)

½ cup/60 g poblano pepper, seeded, stemmed and ripped into 2"/5 cm pieces

⅓ cup/44 g red onion, sliced

Salt

Coarsely ground black pepper

Vegetable oil

Leaves from a sprig of oregano

8 oz/227 g whitefish fillet (we prefer North Atlantic haddock), cut into 4 portions

6 tbsp/89 ml Sauce El Camino (page 216)

¼ cup/60 ml Aioli (page 221) or Cheater Aioli (page 221)

½ cup/44 g The Usual Suspects (page 101)

4 lime wedges

Preheat your oven to 400°F/204°C.

Wrap the tortillas in foil or place in a covered casserole, then pop them in the oven.

In a 9 x 12-inch/23 x 30 cm oven-safe casserole dish, place the poblano and onion. Sprinkle with salt and black pepper, then toss with enough oil to coat. Spread out the vegetables in a single layer and put in the oven. Roast until the onion and pepper are browned, 8 to 10 minutes. Remove from the oven and place the oregano on top of the veg; top with the fish and return to the oven. When the fish is just done, 4 to 6 minutes, remove from the oven and cool a bit.

Add the Sauce El Camino and distribute evenly.

Take the tortillas from the oven and carefully place in 4 stacks (2 tortillas each) on a heated platter. Smear the aioli on the tortillas, then put a piece of fillet on each. Distribute the pepper mixture evenly among the tacos. Ditto for The Usual Suspects. Squeeze lime over the top.

Serve with Tecate in a can. Lime, too.

FARM OCEAN TREE

This is the dish that won us first place in the Farm-to-Table competition at the annual Harvest on the Harbor festival in Portland. Every ingredient we used is from Maine: pork belly from Terra Optima Farm in Rockland, clams from the local flats, apple cider from Sewall Orchard in Lincolnville, sea salt from Marshfield, and the best butter I've ever had from Casco Bay Butter. Everything else was grown right at Headacre Farm. A dish like this shows how a hardscrabble region can yield the most delicious bounty, if you're willing to look for it. As you've probably gathered, I don't fetishize regional authenticity in my cooking, but I do think there is something special about a meal whose ingredients grow within miles of one another. This one highlights the three pillars of Maine agriculture: the field, the orchard and the sea.

SERVES 1 TO 2

8 oz/227 g pork belly

½ onion, sliced thinly

2 cloves garlic, peeled

1 bay leaf

1 tsp sea salt

¾ cup/177 ml cider

6 tbsp/100 g butter

5 leaves kale

2 sour apples, halved and cored

1 sprig thyme

6 littleneck clams, thoroughly washed

Heat a 6-inch/15 cm heavy skillet over medium-high heat. Brown the pork belly well on all sides and remove from the heat. Add the onion, garlic, bay leaf, salt and cider to the skillet. Cover and return to the stove. Lower the heat to medium-low or low, to keep the contents below a boil. Cook for about 2 hours, or until the pork is fork-tender. You can do up to this point a day or two ahead and store it in the refrigerator.

Preheat your oven to 400°F/204°C.

Melt 2 tablespoons/28 g of the butter and liberally brush the kale with it. Set aside.

Remove the pork belly from the skillet (or refrigerator), reserving all the vegetables and liquid. Place the pork belly and apples (core side up) in a 9-inch/23 cm oven-safe casserole dish or skillet. Evenly distribute the remaining 4 tablespoons/57 g of butter over the pork and inside the apples. Roast the pork and apples for 45 minutes, until the pork is thoroughly heated and the apples are soft and light brown.

Add the reserved liquid and vegetables to the casserole. Add the thyme sprig and submerge. Surround the pork with the clams. Cover the entire dish with the kale leaves. Return to the oven and cook for 30 minutes, or until the clams are fully open and the liquid is heated.

Serve to great acclaim.

SQUASH RISOTTO WITH ROASTED KALE

On a 12°F/−11°C day last winter, I met with our farmer, Anne Perkins, to plan the next season's plantings. I got thinking about how these kinds of meetings have been happening at the farm for so many generations. The Benner family owned the place from the '40s through the '90s, and after I moved in their friend Ben, my 85-year-old neighbor, continued to store his carrots, squash, onions and potatoes in the basement next to the cistern. We're now planning to grow more storage crops, which we'll be storing in the same place.

Talking over all those hardy vegetables gave me a hankering for this Squash Risotto, which is a perfect comforting, hearty, vegetarian meal for a cold winter's day. I think plain risotto should usually be served as an appetizer or side, as after a few bites the uniform texture and gentle flavor lose their appeal. Adding squash and kale, however, creates a variety of tastes and textures that stays delicious to the bottom of the bowl.

SERVES 1

2 cups/60 g kale or hearty greens, stemmed, tossed in olive oil

1 cup/137 g winter squash, peeled, seeded and cut into 1"/2.5 cm cubes

½ cup/66 g onion, sliced

4 cloves garlic

1 bay leaf

Salt

Coarsely ground black pepper

1½ cups/255 g parcooked Risotto (page 109)

2 sprigs thyme

Preheat your oven to 450°F/232°C. Put the rack in the middle. Spread the kale on a cookie sheet.

In a 4- to 5-quart/4 to 5 L heavy-bottomed pot, place the squash, onion, garlic and bay leaf. Cover with water. Sprinkle with salt and pepper. Bring to a boil, then lower the heat to a simmer. Cook until the squash is fork-tender, 10 minutes or so. Strain, reserving 2 cups/475 ml of liquid. The rest of the water is a good start for a vegetable stock.

In the same pot, add the rice to the squash mixture, with enough of the reserved liquid to just cover. Bring to a simmer over medium-low heat. Stir constantly, but gently so that you don't destroy the chunks of squash entirely. Some will deteriorate, which will flavor the rice.

As the water disappears, keep adding more, just to cover. Keep stirring to develop that risotto creaminess.

When you've used up half of the water, pop the greens into the oven. Cook them until light brown on the edges and the color has brightened up, about 8 minutes.

Add the thyme to the rice at this point. When you have run out of water, the rice should be tender, creaminess all around. If not, keep adding liquid, and stir, stir, stir. In the end it should be firm enough that the rice will pile rather than pour.

Pile it onto a warm platter with the kale around the edges. With the woodstove a-crankin, and the best company, it will be delightful.

MAINE WEDDING SPECIAL

As the name suggests, we invented this as a celebratory dish for the many weddings that the coast of Maine plays host to in the summer months. It's a variation of paella, with roasted lobster, chouriço (not chorizo) sausage and mussels, flavored with saffron, orange and tomato. Like any paella, it's a bit of prep but the result is worthy of a very special occasion.

SERVES 4

Olive oil

3 cloves garlic, chopped coarsely

1 sweet onion, cut into large dice

1 rib celery including leaves, chopped

1 large poblano pepper, split, seeded and ripped coarsely

4 oz/113 g chouriço

2 bay leaves

3 ripe tomatoes, diced, or 2 cups/473 ml diced canned tomatoes

½ tsp saffron threads

⅔ cup parcooked Risotto (page 109) or other short-grain rice

2 (1½ lb/680 g) Maine lobsters, still squirming

Juice of 2 fresh oranges (in a pinch use 1 cup/237 ml canned juice, but get the good stuff, with pulp)

½ cup/120 ml fish or lobster stock, or low-sodium natural clam juice

½ lb/227 g mussels, rinsed and debearded

Sea salt

Coarsely ground black pepper

Preheat your oven (or smoker) to 500°F/260°C, or its highest level.

In a wide, oven-safe metal pan, place ¼ cup/60 ml of olive oil, and the garlic, onion and celery. Put it in the oven and let cook, stirring occasionally, until the onion softens, 8 minutes. Add the green pepper. Cook for about 5 minutes, until the color brightens and they turn a bit brown.

Add chouriço, bay leaves, tomatoes and saffron. Cook for 20 to 30 minutes, simmering the "sauce" in the oven. Add the risotto and stir.

Split the lobster from head to tail. Scrape the entrails out of the body and head cavities. Clean the vein in the tail. Crack the claws with the back of a French knife or whack with a meat mallet. (This permits the claw meat to cook in approximately the same time as the tail.) Add the OJ and stock to the sauce. Place the lobster halves on the sauce, spooning some onto all parts of the lobster.

Back to the *forno*. Cook for 10 to 20 minutes, then add the mussels. Cook for about as long again. When it is done, the lobster tail meat will be firm (not dry—that's why you spooned the sauce over it). The mussels will be open and the rice cooked through. Add salt and pepper to finish. The chouriço and the natural brininess of the mussel and lobster juice add salt; do taste it before you salt.

Smelling DELICIOUS! Looking YUMMY!

Serve in the casserole dish with big spoons, claw crackers and picks. Prepare to get dirty!

Did you shout SANGRIA?

6

BREAD, PIZZA AND SANDWICHES

"The bread! Dear lord, the bread!" was the biggest response I got when I put out a call to our customers for the recipes they'd like to see in a cookbook. We use one very simple dough—flour, water, yeast and salt—as the cornerstone of our restaurant, from baskets on the tables filled with focaccia to smoky thin-crusted pizzas topped with every kind of wonderful thing, from the basic cheese and sauce to spicy chicken and cabbage slaw.

The heart of a sandwich is actually on the outside. It's the bread. This chapter includes a Fairground Sausage and a Steak Bomb that reinvent the classic midway treats, delicious hamburgers with surprising toppings, hot dogs taken to new places and, of course, our version of the Lobster Roll. All of them would be good in standard rolls, but in the homemade focaccia that you are about to become expert in, they are out of this world.

Don't stop with the recipes here. Make your focaccia and see where it takes you. Bisect a piece and make French toast, or toast it and add a cream cheese schmear. Make the best stuffing of your life. Do anything you do with bread, and make it incredible.

SOME TIPS BEFORE YOU START

There are a few things you need to be careful about in order to produce wonderful bread and pizza.

Flour: This is your main ingredient, where most of the flavor comes from, and what gives structure to the bread. Use a good brand. I prefer King Arthur's Special, which includes malted barley for flavor. Regular old all-purpose flour works great, too (King Arthur is my favorite). Don't use bread flour; it has too much protein for this recipe. I strongly recommend measuring your flour by weight rather than volume. A cup of flour can weigh anywhere from 4 to 5 ounces/113 to 142 g, depending on the way you scoop it out and how compacted it is. That difference is a big deal in baking, which depends on a precise alchemy between ingredients.

Time: I like speed. I am not a guy who takes things slow, unless absolutely necessary. So believe me when I tell you that here, time is necessary. The dough gets better and better as it sits. If you can, let it rise in the refrigerator overnight (or longer). This is called a retarded rise, and creates a more conditioned dough and a more developed flavor. (I also give instructions for same-day bread, which requires at least 4 hours of rising time.) Time is also the key to shaping and stretching the dough into a thin pizza crust. If you find yourself with dough that fights back and won't stretch into the shape you want, just set it down and leave it for 15 minutes or so. Imagine that you are sending your angry dough to take a walk around the block. Once it's had some time to relax, it will be much easier to work with.

Heat: Crank up your oven to 500°F/260°C (or the given temperature) and let it preheat for a good long time. A pizza stone is a big help, because it absorbs all that heat energy and releases it back into the bread or pizza. It will also help keep the oven temperature more constant. Be sure to put the stone in the oven before you preheat. Be aware that your oven will lose heat when you open the door; do so as little and as quickly as possible. Use your oven light to check on the progress.

Water: Generally, wetter is better; wet, sticky doughs become soft, puffy breads. Unfortunately, wet, sticky doughs make for messy hands and counters, and can be frustrating to work with. This is why stand mixers are helpful for bread baking: They remove the temptation to add more flour in order to make the dough manageable. If you're kneading by hand, do your best to put up with the stickiness and add as little extra flour as you can stand.

There are also some things you don't need to care about. Focaccia is quite forgiving. Unlike a sandwich bread (or a conventional sandwich bread, I should say), the shape doesn't really matter. Make it as "rustic" and "artisanal" as you like. Those big bubbles that would be a problem in other kinds of bread are fine here. In fact, bigger bubbles indicate a softer, springier texture. The flavor is simple so you can mix in or top with whatever herbs you fancy. And there's no tapping on the bottom to see whether there's a hollow sound, whatever that means. The bread is done when the crust is dark. It's that simple.

FOCACCIA

With kneading, time and heat, flour, water, yeast and salt transmogrify into an utterly wonderful food. The outside is deep brown and deeply toasty, perhaps charred in spots, while the inside is soft and puffy, with the subtle flavor that wheat develops over a slow rise. Use it to scoop up dip or make crostini; split it crosswise for a sandwich or toast; use the rounded edges for hot-dog buns (really, try it).

When a recipe is this simple, every ingredient and every step matters. Please read the notes on page 157 before you start. I highly recommend weighing the flour; 2½ cups is 12 ounces, for you Americans who don't feel like doing math.

You can double this recipe for bigger bread or if you want to freeze some dough for later. If you double, pay attention to the visual and texture cues given in the recipe; the dough may take longer to rise and bake. A double batch of dough will still fit comfortably in a standard stand mixer.

MAKES ENOUGH DOUGH FOR 1 PLUMP 10-INCH/25.5 CM FOCACCIA
(ENOUGH FOR 6 PEOPLE IF SERVED WITH DINNER) OR 2 PIZZAS

---

1 cup/237 ml warm water, or more if needed

½ tsp active dry yeast

2½ cups/340 g King Arthur's Special or all-purpose flour

1 tsp coarse sea salt, plus more for sprinkling (optional)

Cornmeal, for dusting

Olive oil

Coarsely ground black pepper (optional)

Place the water, yeast and a few pinches of flour in the bowl of a standing mixer fitted with a dough hook, or a large mixing bowl. Stir, then wait a few minutes to let the yeast dissolve and activate. Add the rest of the flour and the 1 teaspoon of salt and mix on low speed, or with a wooden spoon, until combined. You should have a soft, sticky dough. If it seems at all dry or tight, add up to 2 tablespoons/30 ml of water, one at a time. Err on the side of wet rather than dry. Knead on medium-low speed, or by hand, for 10 minutes. When thoroughly kneaded, the dough will be silky and very stretchy; you should be able to stretch out a small sheet between your fingers until you can see through it. Cover the bowl with a warm towel and place in a warm, undrafty place. Let rise until just about doubled, 2 to 2½ hours.

At this point you can move the dough to the refrigerator, or proceed to the next step. If you are refrigerating, leave it overnight or up to 2 days. Pull it out at least 2 hours before you want to bake it and let the dough return to room temperature.

If you aren't refrigerating, turn out the dough onto a well-floured board. Push with your hands or a rolling pin to a thickness of ¾ inch/2 cm. It doesn't matter what shape. We make them squarish, then stretch them a bit for that artisanal effect. Let rise until almost doubled again, 1½ to 2 hours. During this time, preferably at least an hour before you want to bake, preheat your oven to 500°F/260°C with the pizza stone in it.

(continued)

Dust a pizza peel with cornmeal. This will act like ball bearings, allowing the dough to slide. Carefully transfer the risen dough onto the peel. Brush it with olive oil, sprinkle with salt and pepper if you want to, and slide it off the peel onto your pizza stone.

Bake for 10 to 15 minutes, or until deeply browned. We aren't looking for a nice delicate tan here; the flavor and the color develop together. When done, use the peel to remove from the oven and place on a rack to cool.

When at least mostly cool, slice with a serrated knife. I prefer to cut it crosswise first, then lengthwise into long strips. That way the soft interior is exposed and ready for a dip in olive oil or a smear of butter.

The bread is best on the day it is made. Leftovers can be toasted for breakfast or made into croutons.

PAN METHOD

If you don't have a pizza stone, choose a pan with sides at least 1 inch/2.5 cm in height. A 10-inch/25.5 cm casserole dish works great. After taking the dough out of the refrigerator (or after the first rise, if you aren't refrigerating), brush the pan with 2 tablespoons/30 ml of olive oil. Cover the sides as well as the bottom. Place the dough in the pan, cover, and let it come to room temperature. The dough will spread out and poof up as it warms. This will take an hour or so, depending on the temperature in your kitchen. Once it's warmed up and pliable, use your fingers to stretch it out as evenly as possible. If the dough shrinks back and fights you, let it rest a little while. After 10 or 15 minutes, try again to see whether it has relaxed. If it tightens up again, do the same. Once you've matched the dough to the shape of the pan, more or less, flip the dough over, press it out again and sprinkle with salt and pepper, if desired. Cover and let it rise again until almost doubled, 1½ to 2 hours. During this time, preheat your oven to 400°F/204°C with a rack positioned in the middle.

When the dough has risen, brush it with more oil and sprinkle with salt and pepper, if desired. Pop it into the oven and bake until good and brown. Check halfway through to see what is happening on the bottom (this will be easy if you use a glass pan; otherwise, use a spatula to lift up an edge). If you see the bottom browning faster than the top, lower the heat to 375°F/191°C and reposition the rack closer to the top. Use pot holders and a couple of spatulas to transfer the bread from the pan to a rack to cool. Resist getting the butter out or you'll end up with no bread left for dinner.

VARIATION: PIZZA DOUGH

Once the dough has returned to room temperature, or after the first rise if you aren't refrigerating, divide it in half. On a floured board, use your hands and/or a rolling pin to stretch one ball into an 11- to 12-inch/28 to 30 cm circle. If the dough springs back or tears, set it down and let it relax for 15 minutes or so. A warm room and a patient attitude helps the dough (and the cook) relax. Place the circle of dough on a cornmeal-dusted pizza peel or an oiled cookie sheet. Cover with your preferred toppings and bake at 500°F/260°C until golden.

THE STANDARD PIZZA

Here's the basic recipe, with red sauce and cheese. Make this for the kids or when you just want PIZZA in its elemental simplicity.

10 oz/283 g Pizza Dough (page 159), proofed at room temperature

Cornmeal, for dusting

½ cup/120 ml Latex Marinara (page 218)

Pinch dried oregano

3 oz/85 g whole-milk mozzarella cheese, shredded

1 generous tbsp/14 g Romano or Parmesan cheese, ground

Well ahead of time, preheat your oven to 500°F/260°C. Put the rack on the bottom rung and your pizza stone on the rack.

On a floured board, form the dough into an 11- to 12-inch/28 to 30 cm circle. Dust a pizza peel with cornmeal and transfer the dough onto it.

Spread the marinara on the dough: Using a ladle, drop the sauce in the center of the dough. Using the ladle's bottom, make concentric circles, spreading the sauce more or less evenly across the dough. Leave a ½-inch/13 mm border so you have a crust. The center should have noticeably thinner sauce than the rest, because the toppings tend to flow toward the center, and you don't want it to end up soggy.

Sprinkle the oregano on the sauce. Ditto the cheeses.

Ready?

Slide the pizza onto the preheated stone and bake for 10 minutes, or until it is golden brown and just short of charred. Get that cheese brown and bubbling!

Now it is time to eat, then go for a spin by the Boardwalk in your IROC Z Camaro. YO!

JERRY PIZZA

This one is topped with chicken, Thai chili sauce, blue cheese and mozzarella, then covered with a crispy, fresh Asian-style slaw. I have spent years sneering at those Thai pizzas with whatever—you know, peanut sauce, pineapple . . . but somehow I tell myself that this one is different. It is pretty different. It works. Really, you should try this one.

SERVES 2

---

10 oz/283 g Pizza Dough, (page 159), proofed at room temperature

4 oz/113 g raw chicken breast, cut as small as you can

2½ oz/71 g cheap blue cheese

2½ oz/71 g whole-milk mozzarella cheese, shredded

1½ tbsp/22 ml Sriracha

2 tbsp/30 ml Thai sweet chili sauce

1½ tbsp/22 g sambal oelek

1 cup/88 g The Usual Suspects (page 101)

Preheat your oven to 500°F/260°C or its top temperature, with your pizza stone on the bottom rack.

Form the dough into an 11- to 12-inch/28 to 30 cm circle.

Mix the chicken, cheeses and chili sauces in a bowl. Spread the mixture evenly over the dough. Slide it onto your pizza stone and bake until golden brown, about 10 minutes.

Remove from the oven, cut into 4 slices and top with The Usual Suspects before serving. If you made the salad a while ago, pick up the cabbage and leave the juice behind so your pizza doesn't get soggy. Pile it up in the middle; don't cover the entire pizza. That way, some of it will stay cool and fresh, some of it will do a nice sort of wilting and you will get a variety of textures and flavors on every slice.

SLEEPER PIZZA

In the world of hot-rodding, sleepers are cars that don't look like much but are packing major power under the hood. In the world of pizza, the words *pastrami, artichoke, red onion* and *parsley* conceal the fact that the flavor of this pizza will blow your doors off. All go and no show, as they say.

Our signature tactic for pizza is to mix the cheese with the toppings so that everything is perfectly distributed in each bite. For the calorie conscious, this also has the advantage of reducing the amount of cheese on the pizza. Using just enough for flavor and texture, rather than covering the pizza with a cheese blanket, means that the other ingredients can shine. Artichoke! Pastrami! Onion! Pow!

SERVES 2

10 oz/283 g Pizza Dough (page 159), proofed at room temperature

Cornmeal, for dusting

3 oz/85 g pastrami, sliced

¼ cup/33 g red onion, sliced

1 tsp garlic, minced

2 oz/57 g whole-milk mozzarella cheese, shredded

1 tbsp/11 g Romano cheese, grated

6 canned artichoke hearts, drained and quartered

⅓ cup/27 g fresh parsley, chopped

Olive oil, to coat

Preheat your oven to 500°F/260°C or as high as it will go. If you have a pizza stone, heat it in there from the get-go.

On a floured board, form the dough into an 11- to 12-inch/28 to 30 cm circle. Dust a pizza peel with cornmeal and transfer the dough onto it.

Toss all the other ingredients together in a bowl, adding olive oil to coat. Spread the topping on the pizza.

Use the peel to slide the pizza onto your stone, or place the cookie sheet in the oven.

Bake until well browned on the top and bottom. Fear not! A well-done pizza with cheese just short of burned is the goods.

Atlantic Brewing's Logger Lager sounds swell.

REMEMBER PIZZA

This one is called Remember because it was originally associated with a nice memory, but no one at the restaurant ever seems able to recall how to put it together. It is dead simple: onion, garlic and two cheeses, topped with a fresh, lightly dressed salad. What is so hard about that? Granted, it isn't your typical American pizza, but perhaps it should be. Hot, cold, crunch, a little bit of pleasantly wilted lettuce—and pizza becomes health food, because, look, it's a salad.

SERVES 2

---

10 oz/283 g Pizza Dough (page 159), proofed at room temperature

Cornmeal, for dusting

¼ cup/33 g red onion, sliced

2½ oz/71 g whole-milk mozzarella cheese, shredded

1 oz/28 g blue cheese, crumbled

2 tsp/6 g garlic, minced

Good olive oil

2 cups/60 g mixed field greens

Lemon wedge

Preheat your oven to 500°F/260°C or higher, with your pizza stone on the bottom rack.

Form the dough into an 11- to 12-inch/28 to 30 cm circle. Dust a pizza peel with cornmeal and transfer the dough onto it.

In a bowl, mix together the onion, cheeses, garlic and 2 teaspoons/10 ml of olive oil. Spread the mixture evenly over the pizza. Slide it onto your pizza stone and bake until a beautiful golden brown. Then bake it some more. It should take 10 to 12 minutes.

Remove from the oven and cut into 4 slices.

In a bowl, toss the field greens with a dribble of olive oil and a squeeze of lemon. Pile the salad in the middle of the pizza and serve.

PIZZA WITH SMOKED SALMON, MASCARPONE, CARAMELIZED ONION AND KALE

I invented this one in the early 1990s, when it was a real stretch for folks to wrap their heads around a pizza with no red sauce. Back then, salmon belly was a by-product that I got for 50 cents a pound. Those were the days! Now people have caught on and this product is sought after for its intensity of flavor as well as the health benefits of fish oil. So it isn't cheap, but is worth seeking out. Creamy mascarpone, sweet onions and crispy kale are just the right counterparts to the fish.

SERVES 2

10 leaves kale (enough to cover the pizza)

1 tbsp/15 ml olive oil, plus extra for the kale

1½ oz/43 g mascarpone cheese

1 oz/28 g whole-milk mozzarella cheese, shredded

5 oz/142 g smoked salmon belly, diced small

½ cup/44 g Caramelized Onions (page 220)

2 tsp/6 g garlic, minced

10 oz/283 g Pizza Dough (page 159), proofed at room temperature

Cornmeal, for dusting

Salt

Coarsely ground black pepper

Balsamic vinegar

Toss the kale with a little olive oil, to coat. This should be done as far ahead as possible, so that the oil will tenderize the kale. The oil will also keep it from spoiling, so it's a good idea to wash, dry and oil a big batch and keep it in the fridge all week for lots of uses.

Preheat your oven to 500°F/260°C or as high as it will go. If you have a pizza stone, heat it in there from the get-go.

Mix the cheeses together with the 1 tablespoon/15 ml of olive oil. Combine the salmon, onion and garlic in another bowl.

On a floured board, form the dough into an 11- to 12-inch/28 to 30 cm circle. Dust a pizza peel with cornmeal and transfer the dough onto it.

Tile the dough with the kale. Let some hang over the edges, rusticlike. The cheese mixture is clumpy and won't spread evenly (try if you want), so place it in table-spoon-size piles over the kale. Then spread the salmon mixture over. Sprinkle with salt and pepper. This one will look a little strange, with green poking out through the cheese, onion and stuff everywhere. It will bake to an outrageous deliciousness.

Put it in the oven and bake for 10 to 15 minutes, until the crust is browned (lift up the bottom to make sure it's well browned), and the kale crispy where it pokes through. Take it out and drizzle with a little balsamic vinegar.

This is great stuff for any time but a real killer as an unusual brunch dish. Take a wedge, put a couple of poached eggs on it, add hollandaise. Wow.

CONNIE'S PIZZETTE

This is another recipe inspired by my Nanna Connie. It's basically healthy, homemade junk food: an olive oil–fried dough that can be served either sweet or savory. The pizzette is very versatile, snackable, ready for a nosh in ten. These are made in two stages, first fried and stored until needed, then baked and consumed hot. Connie made these in massive batches and stored them in the cabinet, wrapped in waxed paper or perhaps in a decorative tin. Nowadays I'd recommend plastic wrap or a resealable plastic bag.

These can be topped in any number of ways. Here we'll do a savory version with hard cheese, a dab of sauce and anchovy, and a sweet one with cinnamon sugar.

MAKES 7 PIZZETTES

1 recipe Focaccia dough (page 159), refrigerated overnight or risen once at room temperature

Olive oil

Vegetable oil

SAVORY VERSION

1 cup/240 ml Latex Marinara (page 218)

14 anchovies

7 oz/196 g Romano cheese, grated

SWEET VERSION

1 cup/130 g powdered sugar

4 tsp/10 g ground cinnamon

Divide the dough into 7 equal pieces. Each will be a little under 3 ounces/85 g. Roll into balls and let them relax until they are poofy and almost doubled, an hour or two. This will take longer if you are using cold dough.

Flour a board. Roll out each ball to a disk with a thickness of ³⁄₈ inch/1 cm.

It's fryin' time again. In a 12-inch/30 cm heavy skillet, put equal amounts of vegetable oil and olive oil to get a depth of 1 inch/2.5 cm. Heat over medium-high heat to 375°F/191°C. When the oil is hot, fry the disks in batches until they are light gold on each side. They are going to brown in the oven later. Of course you are going to want to cook the first one all the way and eat it posthaste. That's why there are 7 to begin with. Now you have a nice even half-dozen.

Let cool and wrap well. They can be stored up to a week at room temperature.

When ready to finish, preheat your oven (or toaster oven) to 350°F/177°C.

For the savory pizzette: Spread each pizzette with an even layer of marinara, then top with anchovies and cheese. Brown in the oven, about 10 minutes. Eat at two a.m. Pairing: milk out of the carton.

For the sweet version: Toast the pizzettes, plain, for about 10 minutes, or until well browned. Sift together the ground cinnamon and sugar. Put it into a shaker or mesh strainer. Dust the hot pizzettes with the mixture. This is lovely served with warm maple syrup for a Sunday morning treat, along with the paper and some more milk.

FAIRGROUND SAUSAGE

Agricultural fairs are a ritual of Maine summers. Oh, trashy fried dough, fried pickles, fried everything! Then there are the grills loaded with rings of sausages, peppers and onions. There's that wonderful smell. Now, really, the food never seems to deliver on the smell. The onions will be undercooked, the sandwich dry. This sandwich—a sausage roll loaded with peppers, onion, cheese and sauce—came out of a desire to realize the potential of this unglamorous, unsophisticated, delicious, delightful food.

SERVES 1

¼ cup/30 g poblano pepper, seeded and torn in ¾"/2 cm chunks

¼ cup/30 g red bell pepper, seeded and torn in ¾"/2 cm chunks

¼ cup/33 g red onion, sliced

Olive oil

Sausage! 1 (4 oz/113 g link) (Italian. Hot.)

¼ cup/59 ml Latex Marinara (page 218)

2 tsp/6 g garlic, minced

Salt

Coarsely ground black pepper

Leaves from 2 sprigs oregano

¼ cup/33 g whole-milk mozzarella cheese, shredded

2 tbsp/22 g Romano cheese, shredded

Focaccia (page 159)

2 tbsp/20 g hot pickled banana pepper rings (optional)

Preheat your oven to 450°F/232°C. We are going to be roasting rather than grilling the ingredients.

Toss the peppers and onion in olive oil and spread them out on a cookie sheet in a single layer. Put the sausage on the sheet as well. Roast for about 20 minutes. Take a peek: You ought to see some frying action. When the sausage is brown, remove it and place on a plate (you will want to keep the juices). Let the vegetables keep cooking.

Once the sausage has cooled, cut it into quarters lengthwise, so you have 4 wedges. Slice those into ¾-inch/2 cm triangles. Return them to the oven to cook for another 5 minutes. Stir the vegetables. Are they brown? That's good.

Heat up your marinara.

When the vegetables and meat are all well browned, remove from the oven and mix in the garlic. Let them calm down for a few minutes, then stir it all together. Sprinkle with salt and pepper. Add the oregano leaves. Put the marinara on top, then the cheese. Surprise! Put it back in the oven. Let the cheese brown, which should take 8 to 10 minutes.

Remove and let rest a few minutes.

Take your piece of focaccia and cut off a corner (or edge, if it's round) piece, about 8 inches/20 cm long and 3½ inches/9 cm wide. Think of it as a boat for your sausage. The crust on the bottom will prevent blowouts. Slice the boat open, leaving the bottom intact. Fill it with the sausage and vegetables. Top with banana pepper, if using.

Serve with Coke, in a glass bottle, on a summer's eve.

LOBSTER ROLL

The lobster roll is ubiquitous in Maine, served from roadside stands and carts and restaurants of every stripe. Even McDonald's offers lobster rolls in the summer. It had never occurred to me to ask about the origins of this sandwich until our photographer, Stacey Cramp, mentioned that she thought it was invented right here in Rockland. The story goes that Carl Simmons, who had been a lobsterman, opened up a lunch counter in the 1920s, serving fifteen-cent rolls filled with lobster and mayonnaise. A 1953 article in the *Courier-Gazette* (still one of our local papers) also credits Simmons with pioneering the very concept of the lunch counter, and with being the first person to demand mayonnaise in gallon jugs. Who knew that our little town had made such a mark on the world!

The best lobster rolls are simple, but this one does make some improvements on the traditional version. Instead of a hot-dog roll, it's served in a chunk of crusty focaccia, which adds real chew and flavor. There's a sprinkling of tomato, a leaf of lettuce, a good amount of parsley. And you won't be needing a gallon jug of mayonnaise. You'll make your own garlic aioli. I am going to guess that it will taste even better than Mr. Simmons's original.

SERVES 1

3½ oz/100 g cooked lobster meat

1 tbsp/5 g fresh parsley, chopped coarsely

3 tbsp/45 ml Aioli (page 221) or Cheater Aioli (page 221)

Focaccia (page 159)

1 leaf romaine lettuce

½ small tomato, sliced

Place the lobster, parsley and aioli in a bowl. Mix well.

Cut from your focaccia a chunk that is about 6 inches/15 cm long and 3½ inches/ 9 cm wide. If you have a 10-inch/25 cm round, you can cut a quarter from it instead. Split it open to make room for the lobster, leaving the edge crust intact.

Line the focaccia with the romaine. Put in the lobster, with the sliced tomato on top. Serve with hand-cut fries and a small salad, for the full effect.

STEAK BOMB

A good drippy, elbow-wetting, finger-licking, chin-shining, greasy, moist sandwich is a sensual pleasure. This is a sort-of-sub, and it has everything a sub needs, in my opinion: steak, peppers, mushrooms, onions, cheese. It's especially perfect after a night out. This is not to be consumed behind the wheel. *Officer, the olive oil . . .*

SERVES 1

2 tbsp/9 g mushrooms, smashed

¼ cup/42 g poblano pepper, seeded and ripped into 1"/2.5 cm pieces

¼ cup/42 g red bell pepper, seeded and ripped into 1"/2.5 cm pieces

¼ cup/30 g red onion, sliced

5 oz/142 g shaved steak, chopped roughly

4 leaves basil

2 tsp/6 g garlic, minced

½ cup/60 ml Latex Marinara (page 218)

¼ cup/33 g mozzarella cheese, shredded

2 tbsp/22 g Romano cheese, grated

Focaccia (page 159)

2 tbsp/20 g hot pickled banana pepper rings

Preheat your oven to 400°F/204°C.

Toss the mushrooms, peppers and onion in olive oil and spread them out on a cookie sheet in a single layer. Roast for about 20 minutes. Add the steak and cook for 5 minutes more, until cooked through.

Add the basil and garlic to the vegetables. Top with the Latex, then the cheeses. Return to the oven to brown the cheese well.

Take your piece of focaccia and cut off a corner (or edge, if it's round) piece, about 8 inches/20 cm long and 3½ inches/9 cm wide. Split the soft part down the middle, leaving the edge intact. Shovel the filling into the bun and top with banana rings.

Arm yourself with multiple napkins. Resist the fork and knife. Chianti in an old jelly glass would be the traditional bev.

BURGERS

Here is a recipe for the perfect hamburger, guaranteed to win those beer-fueled backyard arguments forever. You will be the hamburger champion. Burgers are simple, red-blooded comfort food, but there are a lot of elements that go into making them really excellent. The directions follow, as well as some suggestions for standout toppings. The recipes are per person; scale up to match your crowd.

The beef really matters. It has to be fresh, and it has to have fat in it. Look for an organic Angus with 20 percent fat. It will say 80/20 on the package. If you have a butcher who will grind to order, have her toss in 5 percent bacon with your beef. You will never be the same.

These can be cooked on a grill or in a cast-iron pan on the stovetop. I prefer the cast-iron: It's easy to get and keep hot, and gives an even sear. The grill does flavor the burgs in a special way, though. If you have a gas grill, you can get some great smoky flavor by soaking some wood chips for an hour or so, then putting them on the grill stones right before the burgers go on. Use a few chips per burger, and close the lid for a few minutes during cooking.

A burger is a sandwich and the bread is what makes it great. That's why I recommend using our Focaccia (page 159). If you don't have time to make it and want to use a standard burger roll instead, make 5-ounce/142 g patties that are ¾-inch/2 cm thick, and be careful not to overcook.

SERVES 1

FOR EACH BURGER

8 oz/227 g organic Angus beef, ground

Worcestershire sauce (preferably Lea & Perrins brand)

Vegetable oil

4½"/11 cm square of Focaccia (page 159)

Form the meat into a patty, 1½ inches/4 cm thick. Feel free to make it square instead of round. Whatever you do, don't fondle the meat. The more you handle, squish and mush it, the worse your burger will be.

Find a shallow container that will fit all your hamburgers. Put in ⅛ inch/3 mm of Worcestershire sauce and put the burgers in it. Let sit at room temperature for 10 minutes, then flip and soak for 10 minutes on the other side. (For those who remember the Sizzle Burger recipe on the bottle of French's Worcestershire Sauce, I am busted.)

Heat your grill or pan to scorching-hot.

If you're cooking on the grill, put a thin layer of vegetable oil in another container and give the burgers a quick dip in it just prior to cooking them. If you are cooking on cast iron, skip the oil.

Put the burgers on the grill or in the pan. Don't fuss with them. You are only going to turn once. You'll see the cooking advance up the side of the burger as the color changes. When it gets about a third of the way up the side, turn the burger. When the side is brownish-gray, you have a medium-rare burger. This might take 3 minutes. If you want your burger done medium, wait until the color gets closer to halfway up before turning, around 4 minutes. If you want it well-done, let it go three-quarters of the way up, 6 minutes. These time estimates will give you a ballpark, but you need to keep a close eye on the color in order to get the doneness you want.

Let them get brown. Seeing smoke? That's normal and good. Don't worry—you almost can't mess this up. The time will vary more on grills, but don't let it go more than 10 minutes total unless hockey pucks are your goal.

If you want to know, chefs have a different method for testing doneness. We poke the meat. You can try it at home. Ready your index finger. Poke a raw burger. It's mushy, right? Try it a few times as the burger cooks. After you turn it over, poke the edge. It will be springy. Poke the middle. It will be softer. So the edge is more done than the center. Take it off the grill when you think it's done and chomp. Then use your brain to coordinate the way it feels with the way of taste. There is some trial and error involved, and good luck if you happen to be a bit beer-addled.

Once your burgers are done to your liking, remove them from the grill or pan. Put each on a bun, top with your favorite things and eat.

BURGER TOPPINGS

I gotta say, personally I find raw onion, Cheddar and ketchup hard to beat on top of a burger. However, I do enjoy a lot of unusual combos. The burger is a perfect canvas to paint a rainbow of flavors for your lucky palate. *Bold* is the go word: The toppings have to be strong enough to defend themselves against the full flavor assault of the burg.

Fair warning: One napkin will not suffice for these burgers.

A little tip: I know I said "toppings," but realize that you can put stuff UNDER the burger! Radical! Do this with cheese. Put it on the bottom of the roll and let the heat of the burg melt it while leaving it with its dignity. This works great with crumbly cheeses, like blue.

All of the following are for one burger and each assumes that you are using a 4½-inch/8 cm square of focaccia for a bun. If you are not, you may need to scale down the toppings somewhat.

BRUTUS BURGER

Crisp lettuce, red onion, red pepper and a zippy creamy dressing. Go.

SERVES 1

---

2 leaves romaine lettuce

¼ cup/60 ml Brutus Dressing (page 41)

⅛"/3 mm slice of red onion

Burger (page 174)

½ roasted red pepper (or enough to cover the burger)

Coarsely ground black pepper

Put one romaine leaf on the bun, then half of the dressing. The onion comes next, with the burger on top. Spread the remaining dressing on the burger and top with the roasted red pepper, a generous grind of black pepper, the other lettuce leaf and the top of the bun.

ROASTED MUSHROOM AND GREENS BURGER

This uses Oven-Roasted Kale (page 92). Put some on the burger and serve the rest as a healthy side. The chew, char and tang of the kale are perfect complements to smoky beef.

SERVES 1

4 leaves, 3 mushrooms and a few onions from Oven-Roasted Kale (page 92)

Balsamic vinegar

Burger (page 174)

Coarsely ground black pepper

Sea salt

Put half of the greens mixture on the bottom of the roll and drizzle with balsamic. Put on the burger, then the rest of the greens. Give it another balsamic drizzle and a sprinkle of pepper and some sea salt. Top with the bun.

MEXI BURG

If you've made some of the Components from this book (see pages 211–224), you're ready to go for this burger. It is soooomessy good. Dirty sweet, as the song says.

SERVES 1

2 tbsp/30 ml Sauce El Camino (page 216)

¼ cup/60 ml Black Bean Ragout (page 212)

Burger (page 174)

2 tbsp/11 g The Usual Suspects (page 101)

1 tbsp/15 g ricotta or other fresh cheese

Heat up the El Camino and ragout while you are cooking the burger. Spread The Usual Suspects on the bottom roll and pour the El Camino into the middle. Add the burger and put the ragout on top. Put the cheese in the middle and squish with the lid.

LAMB BURGER

This is an unusual variation on the burger. With all those vegetables, you can almost fool yourself into thinking it is healthy! And it is, at least relatively speaking. It is basically the sandwich version of Sorta Kefta.

SERVES 1

BURGER
7 oz/198 g ground lamb

Pinch cumin seeds, toasted

⅓ cup/30 g fresh parsley, chopped

1 tbsp/9 g garlic, minced

Salt

TOPPINGS
4 medium leaves spinach, stemmed, tossed in olive oil

⅛"/3 mm slices of ripe tomato, enough to cover the lambsy divey

1/16 tsp Secret Spice (page 224)

6 (⅛"/3 mm) slices cucumber

2 tbsp/30 ml yogurt

Wedge of lemon

1 tbsp/5 g fresh parsley, chopped

Heat a 9-inch/23 cm cast-iron skillet over medium-high heat. Mix the first 5 ingredients together and shape into a patty. Cook to medium-rare, 5 minutes or so per side.

While the lamb is cooking, put the spinach and tomato on the bottom of the bun. Dust the tomato with the spice. Retrieve the burger. Onto the tomato it goes. Put on the cuke and a blob of yogurt.

Put the top on sort of sideways to reveal the interior a little. Squeeze the lemon over everything (the lid, too). Give it a random sprinkle of parsley.

A good, basic Pilsner is a crisp complement.

SURF AND TURF TUBE STEAKS

This hot-dog oddity may not sound like a top choice to everyone, but trust me. It is soooo good! It's just hard to explain the delight that is crab salad on top of a hot dog. Eating this on the patio on a hot Maine summer day (it happens) with an Oxbow Farmhouse Pale Ale cannot be beat. Surf and Turf it is, redneck style.

SERVES 1 TO 2

Vegetable oil

2 hot dogs (we use Pearl brand)

4 oz/113 g cooked crabmeat

3 tbsp/45 ml Aioli (page 221) or Cheater Aioli (page 221)

2 tsp/3 g fresh parsley, minced

Focaccia (page 159)

2 leaves romaine lettuce

½ tomato, sliced ½"/1.5 cm thick

Heat a heavy 6-inch/15 cm skillet over medium heat. Pour in enough vegetable oil to coat the pan with ⅛ inch/3 mm. You are going to panfry the dogs, low and slow. Fry them for 5 minutes, until heated through. You do not want them to brown too much—they should be just a shade darker than raw.

Mix the crab, aioli and parsley.

Slice off 2 corners or edge pieces from your focaccia. Each should be about 6 inches/15 cm long and 3 inches/8 cm wide. You know, like a hot-dog roll. Split it down the middle, leaving the edge crust intact, to make a bun.

Lay a romaine leaf in the bottom of each roll. This will keep them from getting sogged out. Line with the tomato. Place the dogs in their new home. Top with the crab.

Serve with fries, salad and beer.

REUBEN'S LONG-LOST COUSIN

This is a hot pastrami with Swiss cheese, sauerkraut, red onion, our "Ranch" dressing and hot mustard. Is it on rye? No, of course not. It is on our Focaccia. It's delicious that way.

Morse's Sauerkraut down the road makes an absolutely incomparable product. Get it if you can. If not, use any good-quality kraut.

This one requires a LOT of napkins.

SERVES 1

2 tbsp/15 g red onion, sliced

5 oz/14 g red pastrami, sliced (Don't use lean pastrami or the turkey kind.)

¼ cup/57 g good sauerkraut

2 slices of Swiss cheese

Focaccia (page 159)

2 tbsp/30 ml Miranda's "Ranch" Dressing (page 61)

1 tbsp/15 ml Patio Mustard (page 223) or hot mustard

Preheat your oven to 400°F/204°C. Toaster ovens are a charm for this.

Use a small casserole dish. Line the bottom with the sliced onion. Pile the pastrami on top of it, then half of the kraut. Top with the cheese, then the rest of the sauer- kraut. This way, half of the kraut flavors the pastrami, and the rest keeps the cheese from burning. OK, into the oven. Cook it for 8 minutes or so. The pastrami and kraut should be hot, the cheese gooey.

Cut off a chunk of focaccia from the edge or corner of your bread. It should be about 7 x 4½ inches/18 x 11 cm. Split it in half, crosswise.

Smear the ranch on the bottom of the focaccia. Put the pastrami mixture on top. Smear the mustard on the bottom of the lid. Serve with a half-sour or dill pickle and Dr Brown's Cel-Ray.

PHD HOT DOG

I tell folks that I am a PhD: Professor of Hot Dogs. Who doesn't like a hot dog? Yeah, vegetarians. When I was a veg, I did make the occasional exception for dogs from the Coney Island in Pottsville or the Squeeze Inn in Shamokin. Not that I am trying to tempt you from your food ethics and preferences, but if you are going to have a hot dog, try it this way.

This is a nod to the Chicago-style dog. Now, don't go off on me. No, it's not authentic. We can't get the nifty nuke-green relish or those cool peppers, not to mention those rolls! But laying the pickle slices alongside the dog—that's genius. Our "Ranch" dressing carries similar flavors to the Chicago dog toppings, at least if you haven't had a real one in a while. And, of course, no ketchup!

SERVES 2 IF THEY WANT 1 DOG, SERVES 1 IF YOU EAT 2 BY YOURSELF. MY PHD IS NOT IN MATH.

Vegetable oil

2 hot dogs (I use Pearl brand)

Focaccia (page 159)

2 leaves romaine lettuce

½ tomato, sliced ⅛"/3 mm thick

1 tbsp/15 ml Patio Mustard (page 223) or regular hot-dog mustard

2 pickle slices, ⅛"/3 mm thick, cut the long way

¼ cup/60 ml Miranda's "Ranch" Dressing (page 61)

2 tbsp/15 g red onion, sliced thinly

Heat a heavy 6-inch/15 cm skillet over medium heat. Pour in enough vegetable oil to coat the pan with ⅛ inch/3 mm. You are going to panfry the dogs, low and slow. Fry them 5 minutes, until heated through. You do not want them to brown too much—they should be just a shade darker than raw.

Slice off 2 hot dog–size edge or corner pieces of focaccia, about 6 inches/15 cm by 3 inches/8 cm. Split them open to make buns. Leave the edge crust intact.

Lay a romaine leaf in the bottom of each bun. Chef's tipksi: This will help keep your bun intact so it does not disintegrate before you are done eating. Place the slices of tomato along one side of the bun, inside the lettuce leaf. Doggies next. Stripe the mustard along one side. Put in the pickle slice so it's next to the dog. Top it all with the dressing, then the onion.

Go stand outside in the wind and pretend it's Chi-town.

7

PARTY FOOD

The best way to enjoy food is with a crowd of friends, whether on the patio on a summer evening or on the couch in front of a game in the winter. This chapter offers highly shareable snacks that will start conversations, build good cheer and leave your guests with a high opinion of your cooking and your creativity. Some are elegant enough for formal occasions—there are three different lobster cocktails, and several forms of fritters that you can plausibly call croquettes—and some are casual and comfortable, like the Deconstructed Nachos and the NASCAR Pâté, made from leftover meat loaf. Most of the recipes are written for one or two servings so you can easily scale them to the size of your gathering. Fill up a cooler (or decant your wine), pile up a few platters and party!

GUACAMOLE À LA KR

A lot of guacamoles have tomato or salsa blended in with the avocado. Then they are served with salsa on the side. Department of redundancy department. This one puts it all together so all the flavors and textures of roasted corn and peppers are part of the guacamole, and so every single bite is interesting and delicious. Serve it on its own with chips, or as a saladlike accompaniment to a meal.

SERVES 4

1 ear of corn
Olive oil, for brushing
Salt
Juice of ½ lime
2 tsp/10 ml pickled pepper juice
¼ tsp ground coriander, toasted
3 sprigs cilantro, minced
2 ripe avocados
2 tbsp/17 g pickled hot red peppers, seeded and cut into ½"/1.5 cm dice
Tortilla chips, to serve

Heat your broiler. Shuck the corn and remove the corn silk. Brush the corn with oil, just to coat. Sprinkle it with salt. Place on a sheet pan or cookie sheet. Into the broiler! This requires constant vigilance. Let the corn brown, turning so that it cooks evenly. When browned all over, about 8 minutes total, remove from the oven. Let cool enough to handle, then cut off the kernels.

Mix the lime juice, pepper juice, coriander and cilantro together in a bowl. Scoop out the avocado and add it to the bowl. Mash it up. I use a potato masher, which leaves some texture in the dip. Fold in the peppers.

Serve with tortilla chips.

DECONSTRUCTED NACHOS

This dish was the solution to a Cafe Miranda problem. We all love nachos (who doesn't love nachos?), but we couldn't make them in our wood-fired oven. It turns out that 800°F/427°C will combust your chips. So we came up with this deconstructed way of eating them: beans and cheese in a casserole, with chips to dip in it, salsa on the side. Our customers wanted to know what the staff was eating back there, so we had to start sharing with the public.

SERVES 2 TO 3

14 corn tortillas, or a bag of tortilla chips

Vegetable oil

½ lime

¾ cup/177 ml Black Bean Ragout (page 212)

2 slices Cheddar cheese

1½ oz/43 g ricotta cheese

1 sprig oregano (or a pinch dried, if you have to)

1½ oz/43 g mozzarella or Jack cheese, shredded

1 poblano pepper, seeded and cut into large random pieces

¼ red onion, sliced thinly

1 jalapeño pepper, split from stem to tip, not seeded

If making chips: Cut the tortillas into chip-size wedges. Fry until crisp in vegetable oil heated to 350°F/177°C (if the oil is smoking, it's too hot). Stir to keep them from sticking together. It will take about 5 minutes. Drain on paper towels.

Squeeze the lime over the chips, whether you make your own or use a bag.

Spread the ragout in a 9-inch/23 cm oven-safe casserole dish. Top with the Cheddar, ricotta and the oregano sprig, then cover with the mozzarella. Place the poblano pieces around the edge of the casserole, shiny side up. Sprinkle the onion over, and artfully place the jalapeño halves on top. Brush the vegetables with cooking oil.

Place the casserole under the broiler for about 5 minutes, until the peppers are a little charred, the cheese is bubbling and the beans are hot.

Serve hot (use a trivet!) next to a plate of chips and a bowl of salsa.

KAY SO FUN DEE DOH

This is my take on queso fundido, featuring gooey melted cheese and spicy chorizo. It's a quick, fun (de doh) party appetizer. Use a shallow ceramic casserole, around 10 inches/25 cm wide. If you have one of those heavy brown Mexican ones, with the white edge that looks like it's melting, that will be perfect.

SERVES 2

---

2 oz/57 g queso fresco or ricotta

1 tbsp/15 ml heavy cream

4 oz/113 g whole-milk mozzarella, shredded

2 sprigs oregano

3 oz/85 g Cheddar cheese, shredded

1 poblano pepper, seeded and torn coarsely

1 jalapeño pepper, cut from tip to top

3 oz/85 g chorizo, cut into small chunks

¼ red onion, sliced very thinly

3 tbsp/45 ml olive oil

Salt

Coarsely ground black pepper

A few pinches smoked ancho powder or hot paprika

Tortilla chips, to serve

Preheat your oven to 425°F/218°C.

In the casserole dish, place the queso fresco in the middle in a lump. Pour over the cream and evenly distribute the mozz around it. (Pronounce it "motz," please.) Lay the oregano sprigs on either side of the ball of ricotta and on top of the mozz. Cover it all with the Cheddar.

In a bowl, toss both peppers and the chorizo and onion with the oil. Distribute the mixture on top of the Cheddar in a single layer. Sprinkle evenly with the salt, pepper and ancho powder. The ancho will give the dish what we call a "nice face." You know, like yours.

Into the oven! If you have a convection fan, use it here. Bake until the chorizo is cooked and the cheese is brown and bubbly. This will take more than 5 minutes and less than 10. Remove from the oven.

Be CAREFUL! Hot cheese will peel your skin off.

When the cheese has cooled enough to avoid "pizza burn," put the casserole on an underliner plate and pile the chips on the side. Some fresh Salsa Evelyn (page 224) is a nice accompaniment.

I like a mocktail made with freshly squeezed lime juice, tonic and bitters for a refreshing nonalcoholic beverage.

FETA UP

Baked cheese. Can we miss here? This platter of garlicky, olivey cheesiness is a great icebreaker, and a very tasty one. It's easy to make and share, and very wine-friendly. Just watch out for olive oil dripping on your tie.

SERVES 1 AS A HEARTY APPETIZER, 2 TO 3 AS A PARTY SNACK

3 oz/85 g chunk of quality hard feta cheese

⅓ cup/57 g mixed pitted olives (good ones)

¼ cup/28 g pickled banana pepper rings

3 sprigs oregano

½ red sweet pepper, seeded and ripped into 1"/2.5 cm pieces

1½ tsp/4 g garlic, minced

¼ cup/33 g red onion, sliced

1 ripe Roma tomato, quartered

3 tbsp/45 ml extra-virgin olive oil

½ cup/15 g spinach, stemmed

Focaccia (page 159), to serve

Fire up the oven to 400°F/204°C.

Toss all the ingredients, except the spinach and focaccia, in a bowl to thoroughly coat all the stuff. Dump it all into a presentable oven-safe casserole dish. A 7-inch/18 cm ceramic one works well.

Bake for 20 minutes. The peppers will brown just a bit and the oil will be bubbling. Add the spinach and let it wilt.

Serve with plenty of bread.

STOP AND SMELL THE GORGONZOLA

Gorgonzola ain't like roses. However, I prefer to eat the Gorg. Funny how this works, that something that smells so very . . . *rugged* can taste soooo great!

When served to a party with plenty of focaccia bread, no one will care who cut the cheese.

SERVES 1 SMELLY CHEESE EATER

6 button mushrooms

¼ cup/33 g red onion, sliced

Olive oil

5 cloves Blanched Garlic (page 220)

3 leaves basil

2½ oz/71 g Italian Gorgonzola cheese

Lotsa Focaccia (page 159)

Preheat your oven to 450°F/232°C.

Toss the mushrooms and onion with a little olive oil. Place them in a small casserole and put it in the oven. Roast, stirring occasionally, until the mushrooms are mostly cooked through, 8 minutes or so. Don't burn the onion! Add the garlic and basil. Place the hunk of Gorg on top of the basil. Return to the oven for another 8 minutes, or until the Gorgonzola is mostly melted. Smells . . . good, eh?

Serve with plenty of focaccia and a wine strong enough to defend itself.

CHEF'S TIP: Use Italian Gorgonzola. The domestic versions don't melt the same.

POLENTA PARTY SQUARES

Here's an irresistible nibble made from firm polenta flavored with spinach, blue cheese and garlic. Once you learn the technique, the possibilities are endless. This corn mush could hold ball bearings. Try ground beef, wild mushrooms, ham. You can also cut them into any shape with cookie cutters, so you can serve polenta stars, polenta hearts, polenta palm trees and polenta guitars, whatever suits your gathering.

MAKES 48 SQUARES

12 cups/2839 ml water
1½ cups/344 g butter
3 bay leaves
Pinch salt
1 tbsp/7 g coarsely ground black pepper
3 cups/511 g cornmeal or grits
2 cups/60 g spinach, stemmed and chopped
3 oz/85 g blue cheese
3 tbsp/28 g Blanched Garlic (page 220), minced

Place the water, butter, bay leaves, salt and pepper in the top of a large double boiler. Cover and cook until just short of boiling. All the butter should be melted. Whisk in the cornmeal, and keep whisking for about 10 minutes, until the mixture thickens so much it's hard to stir. Make sure you're scraping the bottom and corners of the pot as you whisk. Once the mixture has thickened to the consistency of cement, cover and lower the heat so the water is barely simmering. Now give your arm a rest and let cook for 30 minutes.

Stir in the spinach, cheese and garlic. Pour the mixture into a 9 x 12-inch/23 x 30 cm baking dish. Place on a rack to cool to room temperature, then refrigerate overnight.

When ready to serve, cut into 1½-inch/4 cm squares, or use your cookie cutter to make a shape that best expresses your inner self. Save the scraps and fry them up for breakfast.

SEARED JALAPEÑOS WITH GOAT CHEESE AND RICOTTA STUFFING

Is it party time? These never fail to get attention. I don't know whether it's the contrast between the bright green color and the white cheese, or just the excitement over seeing poppers done right. They tend to increase beer consumption, too.

These can be made well in advance and kept in the refrigerator. They are best at room temperature, so let them warm up before serving.

SERVES 5 TO 6

2½ oz/70 g soft goat cheese

2 oz/57 g ricotta cheese

2 tsp/1 g fresh oregano leaves

⅛ tsp ground coriander, toasted

3 jalapeño peppers, about 4"/10 cm long

Pinch ancho powder

Mix the cheeses, oregano and coriander.

Split the peppers in half from tip to tip, cutting the stem in half if possible. Scrape out the seeds and the white stuff. I advise gloves for fear of your touching someone or something you may regret.

Heat a 9-inch/23 cm or larger cast-iron skillet over medium heat (bigger is better). Put in the peppers, skin side down. You aren't going to cook them through. They need to stay firm so that you can stuff them. Cook for 2 to 3 minutes, so the part that is in contact with the pan chars a bit and the color brightens. Remove from the pan and let cool.

With those gloves again, fill with the cheese. Sprinkle with the ancho powder. Serve at room temperature.

NASCAR PÂTÉ

A joke: What is pâté? Meat loaf that knows somebody.

Think about it, though: Meat loaf is minced beef or pork, cooked to make it flavorful and tender. Served cold, it's a great bit of charcuterie—especially if you make our smoked version.

This is perfect entertaining food. Make it ahead, serve it cold. It has a catchy name. Who could ask for more? Oh, it is also really good!

SERVES 1

1½ tsp/7 ml prepared mustard

1 (1½"/4 cm) slice of Smoked Meat Loaf (page 132)

2 tbsp/66 g red onion, diced small

½ dill pickle, diced small

2 tsp/3 g fresh parsley, chopped

Saltines or Ritz crackers, to serve

Smear the mustard around the plate (let your inner child free). Put the meat loaf slice in the center. Make teeny piles of the onion and pickle on the points of the loaf. Sprinkle the Elvis Parsley over. Serve with crackers, PBR and Talladega on the TV.

WOO-TANG CLAM

This is a great plate to share. Supple clams and chewy pork strips are steamed in a Chinese-inspired broth that is sharp, garlicky, salty and spicy. It makes an exciting alternative to mussels.

You can find the fermented black beans in the sauce aisle at the Asian grocery. If you don't have fish stock, substitute vegetable stock. Lobster stock is even more delicious.

SERVES 1

8 hard-shell clams (mahogany or similar), well washed

2 oz/57 g pork loin, cut into ¼"/6 mm strips

2 oz/60 ml fermented black bean and garlic sauce

¼ cup/42 g red sweet pepper, seeded and ripped into 1"/2.5 cm pieces

2 scallions, cut on the bias

6 tbsp/90 ml fish stock

3 sprigs cilantro

2 lemon wedges

In a 3-quart/3 L saucepan over high heat, mix the clams, pork, bean sauce, red pepper, scallions and fish stock. Cover and bring to a boil, then lower the heat to keep it at a simmer. Cook until the clams open, about 8 minutes.

Pour into a bowl and top with the cilantro. Give the lemon wedges a squeeze.

BRAVE APPETIZER

This is a tasty throwback to the time when there was no food channel presenting fried testicles and such. We had a series of "brave" dishes that were not about obscure animal or sea-creature parts. Instead, they were designed to push the envelope of what we could get away with, sell and make Miranda style (which is to say, satisfying). This one is mortadella wrapped around crabmeat, which was not typical on the appetizer menus of the early 1990s, and isn't now, for that matter. It was, however, inspired by some traditional foods: paella, Portuguese fish stew and other delicious combinations of seafood and sausage.

MAKES 12 ROLLS

7 oz/20 g Maine crabmeat

¼ cup/60 ml extra-virgin olive oil, plus more

Coarsely ground black pepper

1 tsp lemon zest

¼ cup/20 g fresh parsley, chopped coarsely

12 slices of a good mortadella (never had a bad one, now that I ponder it. Salami will also do.)

12 Focaccia Croutons (page 213)

This is soooo easy.

Gently fold together the crab, the ¼ cup/60 ml of oil, ¼ teaspoonof pepper, the zest, and all but a tablespoon/5 g of the parsley. Try not to break up the crab too much.

Lay the slices of mortadella flat. Divvy up the crab among them and spread it evenly, leaving a finger-width strip on the edge uncrabbed. Roll up into a tube or cone and secure with a toothpick. This is a good use for those fancy ones that have languished in the kitchen miscellaneous drawer all these years.

Arrange the rolls with a pile of croutons on a plate. Sprinkle with parsley and drizzle with olive oil. Then more oil. Sprinkle with pepper. Serve, bravely.

PHISH KAKES

These are good anytime: brunch, luncheon, supper, in sandwiches. They are damn good cold, at midnight. They are great for parties, with a bowl of aioli for dipping. Try serving them as an entrée accompanied by White Bean Ragout (page 213), French fries and a slaw made of cabbage, red onion and our "Ranch" dressing (page 61).

SERVES 4 AS AN ENTRÉE

½ cup/120 ml vegetable oil
¼ cup/30 g celery, minced
½ cup/66 g onion, minced
1 lb/454 g smoked whitefish
3 tbsp/18 g garlic, minced
1 large egg, beaten, plus another if needed
¾ tsp molasses
Salt
Coarsely ground black pepper
1 cup/120 g bread crumbs
1 cup/237 ml Aioli (page 221) or Cheater Aioli (page 221) for serving

In a heavy, shallow 10- to 12-inch/25 to 30 cm pan, heat the oil with the celery and onion over medium heat. Cook to sweat the vegetables, stirring as needed. No browning, folks. In about 10 minutes, the onion will be translucent and sweet. That is what we want. Remove from the pan and chill. Because we are using eggs here, we need the ingredients to be cold, for safety's sake.

In a largish bowl, flake the fish with your hands. Mix in everything else, except the aioli and ½ cup/60 g of the bread crumbs. You should find that the mixture will form a ball in your hand when squeezed. If it doesn't, beat an egg in another bowl. Add half of it to the mixture and try again, then add more if still needed. Chill through.

Preheat your oven to 350°F/177°C.

Heat a 10- to 12-inch/25.5 to 30 cm skillet over medium heat with enough vegetable oil to come up ½ inch/1.5 cm.

Portion the fish mixture into 4 pieces and shape each into a 1-inch/2.5 cm-thick cake. Pat the remaining bread crumbs onto each one to make a crust.

Cook the cakes for 5 minutes or so on each side, to a deep golden cover. Turn them just once. Then toss in the oven for another 8 minutes or so to cook them through.

Serve with the aioli.

This is great with a regional old-school New England brewski, like Narragansett!

FISH HASH

This was one of the very first Miranda dishes: a hash of roasted haddock, caramelized onions, fried sweet potato and roasted greens, topped with eggs and hollandaise. It may be the best brunch dish you will ever eat, but it's good any time of day. I came up with this while working at the East Wind Inn, circa 1988. The late Tim Watts was the owner, and was one of the mentors who got me where I am today. He was, shall we say, a traditionalist. I had a lot of ideas, and he thought they were nuts (correct, Mr. Watts). He kept me on a short leash with regard to supper menus, but let me go at it for brunch. Hence, Fish Hash.

Use the freshest eggs you can get. Yes, always, but with poaching it is crucial so you do not wind up with poached egg yolks when the whites swirl away.

SERVES 2

FOR THE HOLLANDAISE
2 large egg yolks
Salt
Dash Tabasco
½ cup/115 g butter
½ tsp freshly squeezed lemon juice

FOR THE EGGS
5 large local eggs (You only need 2 per person, but you may break one while poaching)
Pinch salt
2 tsp/10 ml freshly squeezed lemon juice

Let's do the hollandaise first. This a total cheater method. Easy, quick and highly idiot-resistant.

In the trusty stand mixer with the whip attached or the food processor with the "S" blade (the regular one), place the 2 yolks, Tabasco and a couple of pinches of salt. Beat until the yolks are pale, like a watercolor yellow.

Meanwhile, place the butter in a microwave-safe measuring cup that you can pour from. Zap it in the microwave to melt and get the butterfat and the whey HOT. As soon as the micro has scrambled the molecules, turn your mixing appliance of choice back on high speed. S L O W L Y pour the butter into the spinning yolks. This should emulsify to a shiny sauce of buttery richness. At the last second, add the lemon and salt. DONE. This is best held in a thermos. Really. I use one of the big-mouth ones that can hold a meal, and it does a great job.

Start the eggs: We are poaching here, so pay attention.

Use a shallow nonreactive pan, perhaps 3 inches/8 cm deep, with a 10-inch/25 cm or larger diameter. Fill with water, leaving some headroom so that it will not overflow when the eggs are added. Add a pinch of salt and the lemon juice. The acid will bind the egg whites so they will stay together. Bring the water to a boil, then lower the heat to a simmer. Cover the pan and leave it for now, without adding the eggs.

FOR THE FRIES

Olive oil

2 sweet potatoes, peeled and cut like fries

FOR THE HASH

1 cup/132 g red onion, sliced

Olive oil

7 oz/198 g fillet of haddock

2 tsp/6 g garlic, minced

3 cups/90 g spinach, stemmed if needed, oiled

Salt and coarsely ground black pepper

Cook the fries: Place ½ inch/1.5 cm of oil in a 12-inch/30 cm skillet over medium heat. Heat until a drop of water will sizzle. Add the sweet potatoes and sauté until tender and starting to brown. Drain on paper towels and keep warm. (You can save time in the morning by making the fries a day ahead and reheating them spread out on a cookie sheet. This works well with any hand-cut, self-cooked fries, not your crinkle-cuts or McD's.)

Preheat your oven to 325°F/163°C. Start the hash: Use a heavy roasting pan or oven-friendly 10-inch/25 cm skillet, and preheat it in the oven. Put the onion in the hot pan with 1 tablespoon/15 ml of olive oil. Let it brown and caramelize in the oven, stirring so that it cooks evenly. This will take about 10 minutes.

Add the fish and garlic. Roast for about 5 minutes more, then stir. It's OK to break up the fillet (we are making hash, after all). Add the spinach and roast until the color intensifies, a couple of minutes more. When you see the color change, remove the pan from the heat and put it on a trivet. Toss in the sweet potato fries and gently stir. Season with salt and pepper. Park it while you cook the eggs.

At this point we need to recognize the skill of multitasking that all cooks, especially breakfast cooks, possess.

Eggs, part 2.

Remove the lid from the pan of simmering water. Adjust the heat so there are just the tiniest bubbles rising. The water temperature ought to be around 205°F/96°C.

Crack an egg into a small bowl that can be submerged in hot water. You do not want to crack them directly into the water as this greatly increases the likelihood of the yolks breaking.

Sliiiiide the egg out of the cup into the simmering water. Easy does it!

Repeat.

Repeat.

Repeat.

And, if you broke one: Repeat.

Let cook until the whites are just set, the yolk still liquid, 6 to 8 minutes, depending on your runniness preference.

Spoon the sweet potato mixture onto the warm platter. Remove the eggs from the poaching liquid with a slotted spoon so the water stays in the pot. Place the eggs on the mixture. Pour the Happy Hollandaise over the whole pile. Grind some pepper.

I heartily recommend a lemonade or grapefruit mimosa as a quirky and sharp counterpoint.

PORK AND SHRIMP CAKES

These are grilled nuggets of ground pork and minced shrimp, great for parties of all seasons. You can also make a more substantial meal of them with panfried noodles, kale and sweet peppers. The pan fry features a zippy chili-lime sauce that is a perfect complement for the meat.

This is a good use for broken pieces of shrimp that you don't want to use in a cocktail. They get chopped up so it doesn't matter what they look like.

SERVES 2

FOR THE CAKES

10 oz/283 g ground pork

8 oz/227 g shrimp, peeled, deveined and cut into small dice

1 tbsp/10 g cooked unsalted peanuts, chopped finely (use the food processor)

1½ tsp/7 ml Thai fish sauce

FOR THE PAN FRY

Vegetable oil

¼ cup/42 g red sweet pepper, seeded and ripped into 1"/2.5 cm chunks

¼ cup/33 g red onion, sliced

1 cup/60 g kale, stemmed, tossed in oil

7 oz/200 g medium rice stick noodles (fettuccine width), soaked overnight and drained

6 tbsp/89 ml sweet chili sauce

2 tbsp/30 ml sambal oelek

¼ cup/60 ml hoisin sauce

6 leaves basil

6 sprigs cilantro

½ lime

Sriracha, for garnish (optional)

Black sesame seeds, for garnish (optional)

For the cakes, get a medium flame going on your charcoal or gas grill. Combine the pork, shrimp, peanuts and fish sauce (the paddle on your standing mixer works great for this). Divide the mixture into 4 equal portions. Shape each into a 1-inch/2.5 cm thick disk. Place them on the grill. Cook, turning once, until just barely done. It will take around 4 minutes per side. You want them medium-rare.

For the pan fry, heat a wok or 12-inch/30 cm skillet over high heat. Coat the bottom of the pan with the thinnest coat of oil. Put in the red pepper and let it brown on one side, 4 minutes. Scooch it to the side of the pan. Add the onion (and a little more oil if the pan is dry). Let cook about 4 minutes to brown that, too. Stir in the pepper. Add the kale and mix it all up. Arrange the noodles on top. This will act like a lid, to steam the vegetables underneath. Let it go about 5 minutes.

OK, this is the tough part. You need to act like a cook and flip it all in the pan. The noodles need to end up underneath the vegetables. Get there however you can. Add more oil if the noodles are sticking. Cover the pan and let the noodles brown, but not char (they will become bitter and wooden if they cook too long). This will take about 6 minutes.

Add the sauces and basil, and cover again for 3 minutes. This will soften up the noodles.

Get a heated platter ready. Slide the pan fry out onto it. Arrange the cilantro over the top. Put the cakes on top and squeeze the lime all over. You can also doll up the edges with some Sriracha squirted on the rim of the plate and a sprinkle of black sesame seeds for color.

CRAB BALLS

Imagine really terrific Tater Tots, but made with sweet potato. Now imagine that they are full of delicious crabmeat. That is the Crab Ball. This one evolved through several permutations, from the idea of a vegetable fritter (which never got off the ground) to mashed potato cakes that disintegrated in the pan, to these sweet, complex, panko-crusted cakes with a sour cream and horseradish sauce. You can substitute cooked winter squash for the sweet potato—just use a volume that matches the crabmeat.

SERVES 2

SAUCE

1 tbsp/15 g prepared horseradish (preferably Morse's brand)

½ cup/120 ml sour cream

Juice of ½ lemon

¼ cup/10 g chives or scallions, chopped

Salt

Coarsely ground black pepper

1 largish sweet potato

1 cup/135 g cooked crabmeat

Leaves from a sprig thyme

Pinch salt

Coarsely ground black pepper

1 cup/100 g panko bread crumbs

Vegetable oil, for frying

Combine the sauce ingredients in a bowl and set aside.

Peel the sweet potato and cut into large chunks. Steam until tender, about 8 minutes. When cool enough to handle, mash. You want 1 cup/225 g of mashed potato, or an amount equal to the crab. Chill before mixing with the crab. You need it to get cold so as to keep everything at a safe temperature.

Combine the sweet potato with the crabmeat, thyme, salt and a grind or two of pepper. Chill the mixture until stiff, about an hour.

Form the potato mixture into four 2-inch/5 cm balls. Roll each in panko to coat.

Heat 1 inch/2.5 cm of vegetable oil in a 12-inch/30 cm cast-iron skillet over medium to high heat to 350°F/177°C (you can also use an electric deep fryer). Drop in the balls and fry for 6 minutes, turning so that they cook evenly, until golden and crispy. Remove with a slotted spoon and drain on paper towels.

Smear the sauce on a plate and arrange the balls on top.

CELLARDOOR LOBSTER COCKTAIL

This dish was created for a dinner at the terrific Cellardoor Winery in Lincolnville, just up Route 1. Cellardoor's wines are elegant and great for pairing. This lobster salad is a classic, with tomato, garlic and bitter greens. We change these with the season, depending on what is growing at Headacre Farm. Mustard, beet or dandelion greens, or baby kale, are all great here.

Commercially picked Maine lobster meat is wonderfully convenient. Given the time it takes to get the meat out of a lobster, it's a bargain, too. Think of it as lump crabmeat with an attitude.

SERVES 1

---

1 generous cup/40 g bitter leafy greens
½ Roma tomato, split stem to bottom
Coarse salt
Coarsely ground black pepper
1 tbsp/15 ml good-quality balsamic vinegar
3 oz/85 g cooked lobster meat
¼ cup/60 ml extra-virgin olive oil
¼ clove garlic, minced

Wash and pat dry the greens. Tear them into bite-size pieces.

Coat the tomato half with salt and pepper. Get out a heavy 6-inch/15 cm skillet or pot. Seasoned cast iron is the ticket if you have it. Heat on medium-high heat, and when hot, place the open, salted side of the tomato in the pan. Now, leave it alone! What we want here is a pan-charred tomato, to re-create the effect of fire-roasting. Let it cook on the same side until charred and soft throughout, 4 or 5 minutes, then remove from the pan and let cool until you can handle it. It doesn't have to be chilled. Warm is cool in this dish. Chop to bite size, and add the balsamic vinegar.

In a bowl, large enough to toss with both (washed) hands, mix together the lobster, greens, oil and garlic.

Use a chilled cosmo glass. Place the tomato mixture in the bottom and top with lobster mixture. Serve on a doily with a teeny fork.

LOBSTER SAMBAL

This lobster cocktail is all about summer. It's spicy, coconutty, crunchy and bright. Serve in chilled martini glasses with spoons, because your guests will want to drink up the delicious juice left in the bottom.

**SERVES 2 AS A HEARTY APPETIZER,
1 AS AN ELEGANT MEAL**

3 oz/85 g cooked, picked Maine lobster meat

1 oz/30 ml coconut milk, at room temperature

1 tsp sambal oelek

4 leaves mint

2 tbsp/13 g mung bean sprouts

Splash of Thai fish sauce

Juice of ½ lime

¼ tsp black sesame seeds, toasted

2 sprigs cilantro

2 lime wedges

Combine the lobster, coconut milk, sambal oelek, mint, mung bean sprouts, fish sauce and lime juice. Scoop into chilled glasses and garnish with the sesame seeds, cilantro and lime wedges.

VACATION IN YOUR MOUTH

Being that my notion of going south in winter means I go to the 'Keag Store in South Thomaston for a bowl of chowder, I get my vacation any old time by eating the foods of warm places. If you want to brighten up a winter party, serve this cocktail of lobster with chile peppers, lime and Asian-inspired flavors. Serve it in martini glasses or in a bowl, with pieces of romaine to scoop up the salad.

If you want extra spice, sub jalapeño peppers or Thai chiles for the poblanos.

SERVES 2

---

4 oz/113 g cooked lobster meat

1 poblano pepper, seeded and minced

2 scallions, green and white parts, sliced on the bias

Juice of 2 limes

2 tbsp/30 ml extra-virgin olive oil

1 tbsp/15 ml Thai fish sauce

6 leaves basil, preferably Thai, shredded

4 sprigs cilantro

¼ cup/44 g Thai bean thread or rice vermicelli noodles, soaked and chopped randomly

GARNISHES

Pinch kimchi flakes

1 tsp black sesame seeds

2 sprigs cilantro

2 thin rounds of lime

10 leaves romaine lettuce

Mix together everything but the garnishes. Spoon the mixture into martini glasses. Make sure to include all the good limey, salty juice. Sprinkle with the kimchi flakes, black sesame seeds and cilantro. Garnish with a lime round on the edge of each glass. Place the glasses on a plate and arrange the romaine leaves around them, attractively. Fill leaves with mixture—crunch!

A nice Moscato with a little bit of sweet goes well with the spicy flavors. Or perhaps enjoy with a nice simple beer such as a Sebago Saddleback Ale.

OYSTERS

Oysters are nothing new as a food source here on the Maine coast. Scattered along the 3,000 miles of coastline are oyster middens: massive deposits of discarded shells. These are the leftovers, the rubbish, of generations of Native Americans enjoying oysters just as we do. That's not to say our oyster supply hasn't evolved in recent years. We now have a wealth of aquaculture projects that are building up the oyster population again. One thing that hasn't changed is that cold water of Maine produces a wonderfully textured briny delicacy.

Oysters are great for a party as they require little prep other than washing them well to remove seaweed, dirt and sand.

As for opening oysters, I suggest finding a friend to do it. I got away for 29 years as a chef without opening an oyster. At the beginning of my career I watched it happening and thought, "Point a knife at my own hand? Not for me." However, in my 30th year as a cook I was doing a catering job and there was no one around who knew how to do it. I escaped unscathed, but if you're going to be opening a lot of oysters, I do suggest getting a Kevlar mesh glove to protect your hand.

Web videos will do a better job of teaching you to open an oyster than I can, so here I'm just going to give some suggestions for toppings to drizzle over raw oysters, as well as a tasty way to cook them up.

For the simplest preparation: Drizzle ⅛ teaspoon of your best extra-virgin olive oil on each oyster. Give them a squeeze of fresh lemon. Sluuuurp!

For more complexity, get a dozen oysters and mix together one of the following:

½ cup/118 ml of freshly squeezed lime juice, 2 tablespoons/20 g of minced red onion and 2 tablespoons/ 10 g of minced fresh parsley

or

½ cup/118 ml freshly squeezed lime juice, 2 tablespoons/10 g of minced scallion, 2 tablespoons/10 g of minced fresh cilantro and (if you like) 1 teaspoon of seeded and minced jalapeño pepper

or

½ cup/118 ml of quality white wine vinegar, 2 tablespoons/20 g of minced shallot and 1 tablespoon/10 g of minced fresh tarragon

Drizzle 1½ teaspoons/7 ml of your chosen mixture over each oyster.

ROASTED OYSTERS

½ cup/60 g spinach, tossed in olive oil and chopped finely

¼ cup/60 ml heavy cream

1 generous tbsp/14 g Romano or Parmesan cheese, grated

1 tsp coarsely ground black pepper

Olive oil

12 oysters, shucked

12 thin (⅛"/3 mm) slices of tomato

Sea salt

Preheat your oven to 375°F/191°C.

Mix the spinach, cream, cheese, pepper and a dab of olive oil. Cover each bivalve with just enough of the mixture to fill the oyster and shell, about a tablespoon and a half. Place a tomato slice on top of each. Brush the tomato with some olive oil and give it a sprinkle of sea salt.

Put them in a shallow casserole large enough to accommodate a single layer and bake for 8 minutes, or until the sauce bubbles.

Serve, of course, with Champagne.

8

COMPONENTS

Cooking from scratch is overrated. Did everyone's eyebrows just go up? What I mean is that every meal shouldn't be made from the rawest of raw materials. Having some components made up ahead and stored in the fridge or freezer means that you can put together a complex meal in a much more efficient way. You don't always have time to stew beans or caramelize onions for a weeknight dinner, but you can do big batches on the weekends. Then, come Tuesday, you can pull out a few bags and have a big head start on a meal.

This chapter includes hearty bean ragouts that serve as soup bases and side dishes; flavor bombs, like caramelized onions and roasted garlic, which multiply the deliciousness of almost anything; and sauces from marinara to aioli. Some of them take time, but none is difficult. Once you start making them you may find that you rely less on cans and jars from the store. In other words, you might cook more from scratch.

LENTIL DOLL

This is our version of an Indian dal, a lentil stew that is used as a dish on its own and as a base for soups and stews. Ours uses garden-variety brown lentils from the supermarket, stewed with aromatics and enlivened by curry powder and Szechuan peppercorns. For a more versatile flavor profile, you can omit the curry and peppercorns.

MAKES ABOUT 8 CUPS/1893 ML

4 cups/800 g dried lentils

Vegetable oil

2 ribs celery, diced medium

6 cloves garlic, peeled

⅔ cup/88 g onion, sliced

1 tbsp/8 g Szechuan peppercorns

2 bay leaves

1 tbsp/6 g curry powder

Salt

Coarsely ground black pepper

Spread out the lentils on a tray and pick over for stones. Then rinse them.

Place a large, heavy saucepan over medium heat, and pour in vegetable oil to a ¼-inch/6 mm depth. Add the celery and garlic. Sauté for 4 minutes, then add the onion, peppercorns and bay leaves. Continue to cook until the onion is clear and sweet, 8 minutes. Add the curry and cook for another 3 minutes, then add the lentils.

Cover with water and bring to a boil, then lower the heat to a simmer. Cover the pot. Cook for about an hour, adding water as needed to keep the mixture barely covered. When the lentils are tender, remove the lid and continue to cook so that some of the water evaporates. This ain't soup (yet). When some of the water has cooked off, season with salt and pepper.

Let cool to room temperature and refrigerate until needed. This will keep for a week in the refrigerator and freezes well.

Use in: Lamb and Lentil Pasta (page 79), Lentil Soup (page 55), Gnu Thing (page 142) and as an accompaniment to Middle Eastern and South Asian foods.

YELLO RICE

This aromatic, bright-yellow preparation of jasmine rice is a staple in my kitchen. It has several advantages: It's quick, highly idiot-resistant, keeps for a week, reheats wonderfully in the microwave and adds a lovely burst of color to a plate. Of course, it also tastes great. The technique of sautéing the rice in oil, then using the oven to finish cooking, adds some complexity and an exotic twist to lots of foods, from burritos to curries, even a basic beans and rice.

You can substitute basmati rice for the jasmine. It will have a fluffier, drier texture.

MAKES ABOUT 6 CUPS/965 G

2½ cups/591 ml water
¾ tsp salt
¼ tsp coarsely ground black pepper
1 bay leaf
⅓ tsp ground turmeric
3 tbsp/45 ml vegetable oil
2 cups/390 g raw jasmine rice

Preheat your oven to 325°F/163°C.

In a 3-quart/3 L saucepan over high heat, bring the water, salt, pepper, bay leaf, and turmeric to a simmer, covered. Lower the heat to keep it simmering.

Put the oil and rice in a heavy, shallow 9 x 12-inch/23 x 30 cm oven-safe casserole that can go on the stovetop, or a skillet that can go in the oven. Over low heat, sauté the rice in the oil, stirring constantly. You do not want any browning. You will see the rice start to change tone, so that it becomes more opaque. This will take about 5 minutes.

Carefully pour the hot water mixture into the pan. Stir it once. Once!

Cover tightly and transfer to the oven. Cook for 20 minutes.

Remove from the oven and uncover. Be careful of the steam. Fluff with a fork.

You can eat the rice now, or let it cool and then refrigerate. Because you fried the rice in oil, it won't clump together in the fridge, and will reheat like a charm.

Use in: Chicken X (page 120), Chicken Jerry (page 117), Veg or Lamb Wowie (page 139), Gnu Thing (page 142), Secret Scallops (page 145), Haddock Enchilada (page 147) or wherever you want rice.

SAUCE EL CAMINO

I'm a gearhead. If you are a gearhead, of a certain age, you may have already understood the little joke of this sauce. From the '50s through the '70s, Ford made a combo car/truck (automotive centaur?) called the Ranchero. Chevy's version, of course, was the El Camino. When I wanted to do a take on ranchero sauce, I knew just what to call it. El Camino is a thick, dark, intense sauce that will add loads of flavor to your Mexican-inspired dishes. Make a lot and freeze it in ice-cube trays for instant spice and complexity.

MAKES ABOUT 2 CUPS/473 ML

¼ cup/60 ml vegetable oil

6 cloves garlic, peeled

6 tbsp/90 g roasted chiles (canned or make your own)

2 bay leaves

⅓ cup/42 g quality chili powder

1½ tbsp/10 g ground cumin

1 tbsp/12 g ground annatto (this gives the rich color)

1 tbsp/5 g ground coriander

2 tsp/2 g dried oregano

2 cups/264 g onion, sliced

½ cup/60 g celery, cut coarsely

½ cup/60 g carrot, peeled and cut coarsely

1 oz/28 g almonds, toasted

¾ cup/177 ml water

Heat the oil in a 4-quart/4 L Dutch oven, wider rather than taller, over medium heat. Add the garlic and toast until golden brown. Add all the spices and the oregano and stir, cooking for about a minute, until the smell is great. Add the onion, celery and carrot. Cover and sweat the vegetables until the onion is translucent and the carrot and celery are fork-tender. This will take about 30 minutes. It's a lot of stuff! Add the almonds and water.

Simmer, stirring occasionally, for at least 2 hours. It can scorch easily, so keep an eye on it. The smell will fill the house and make mouths water!

Remove from the heat and let cool. Puree, using an immersion blender, food mill or food processor. You are looking for a coat-a-spoon consistency. Add more water if necessary.

Use in: Haddock Enchildada (page 147), I Had It in Biddeford (page 24), Pork Mole (page 128), Huevos Miranda (page 144), Oven-Roasted Fish Tacos (page 148) or wherever you need delicious spicy flavor.

MARINATED TOMATO

This method bumps up the flavor of your tomatoes, even the sickly winter ones. Keep it in your refrigerator for several days; it's really handy to have these on hand.

MAKES ABOUT 2 CUPS/473 ML

4 ripe medium tomatoes
Salt
Coarsely ground black pepper
½ cup/120 ml extra-virgin olive oil

Cut the top from the tomatoes and put aside. Dice the rest into ½-inch/1.5 cm chunks. Put in a bowl and salt and pepper them. This will cause the tomatoes to bleed some liquid for the marinade.

Put the tomato tops and oil into a blender. Liquefy them. Pour over the salted tomatoes and stir. Store in the refrigerator until needed.

Use in: Chicken X (page 120), Pasta Chicken (page 118), Secret Scallops (page 145), Wedgie (page 44), Renee's Salad (page 46), White Bean Soup (page 54), Lentil Soup (page 55), Bacon/Tomato/Peas Pasta (page 73), Lamb and Lentil Pasta (page 79), Connie's Old School Pasta (page 82) . . . really, anywhere.

ROASTED GARLIC CLOVES

Slow-roasting garlic transforms it into a sweet, creamy, spreadable item. You can eat a whole head and not be peeling paint with your breath. You'll end up using this not only in the recipes in this book, but in all sorts of things. It's great added to soups and sauces, or just spread on focaccia. Make a big batch as this keeps for quite a while.

If you can find whole peeled cloves, packed dry (not in oil), it will make life somewhat easier.

½ CUP/160 G

1 cup/160 g whole cloves garlic, peeled
Olive oil

Preheat your oven to 325°F/163°C. Choose a pan that can accommodate all the cloves so that they are close together but not overlapping much.

Coat the garlic cloves with oil, put them in the pan and add more oil so that it is ¼ inch/6 mm deep. Cover the pan with an oven-safe lid or foil.

Roast, covered, for at least an hour. The happy cloves are slooooow cooking to that sweet place. After an hour, give the cloves a poke. They should be uniformly soft and sweet.

Remove the cover and continue roasting. All of that slow cooking has left you with starches that will now caramelize to sugary tastiness. Let cook for another 10 or 15 minutes, stirring gently to brown evenly. You are looking for a light or caramel brown.

Let cool to room temperature and refrigerate, covered in oil. Use the garlic-infused oil as a delicious dressing for hearty greens!

LATEX MARINARA

This isn't my grandmother's marinara recipe, but it's inspired by her chunky, unrefined cooking. Kids had two jobs in the kitchen when she was making sauce. We squeezed tomatoes and grated cheese. You didn't want to be on cheese grating, and you didn't want to think much about what might be in the cheese you ate later. Nanna Connie made her sauce rough and chunky, which you can do with this recipe, or you can pass it through a food mill to make it smooth.

Why is it called Latex? It got that name long ago, when the restaurant was half-built and I'd made the first pot of sauce. I was putting it away while talking over paint choices, and the container of sauce got labeled "latex." The name stuck, though it might be more accurate to call it oil-based.

Note that when recipes call for Latex, I mean the smooth, food-milled version.

MAKES ABOUT A QUART/946 ML

---

6 tbsp/90 ml olive oil

4 whole cloves garlic

½ cup/66 g onion, sliced thinly

Pinch ground cloves

28 oz/794 g canned tomatoes

2 tbsp/34 g tomato paste (optional)

Salt

Coarsely ground black pepper

Heat the olive oil in a heavy, nonreactive 3-quart/3 L pan over medium-high heat. Add the garlic and toast until golden, 3 or 4 minutes. Add the onion and let it sweat about 6 minutes, until translucent, sweet and soft. Add the cloves. Simmer for 5 minutes. Dump in the can of tomatoes.

Simmer for an hour and a half, until the tomatoes break down. If necessary, mash with a potato masher (the wavy kind will work better than the grid kind). Taste. It will be highly acidic. Add salt to taste, which will neutralize the acid. There's no need for sugar. If the texture is too loose or the flavor too thin, stir in the tomato paste. Add pepper to taste.

Leave it chunky if that's what you like. Otherwise, put the sauce through a food mill. Don't use a food processor; you need to get the seeds out or the sauce will be bitter.

This keeps for weeks and freezes well.

BLANCHED GARLIC

This technique gives garlic a mature, cooked, sweet flavor that is clean and mellow. While there's no caramelization, as there would be if you sautéed or roasted the garlic, this method removes the bite from both the garlic and the eater's breath. It really makes garlic quite genteel. You can use the whole cloves for a head start in a roasted dish or mince them and add to a dish at the finish.

See whether your produce folk can get you a pound/450 g of commercially peeled cloves. Otherwise, you'll have to peel all those cloves. You need to keep them intact, so you can't use any trick that involves smashing. You can use this one: Cut the hard end off each clove and toss them all into a pot of water. Reach in and rub the cloves vigorously between your hands. The water will make the skins less sticky, and the cloves will sink while the skins float. You are welcome.

---

1 LB/450 G

---

1 lb/450 g whole cloves garlic, peeled
4 cups/500 g ice

Boil water in a 5-quart/5-liter pot. You need enough water to cover the cloves by ½ inch/1.5 cm. Once boiling, reduce the heat to a simmer. Add the cloves and cook for 10 minutes, or until the cloves are soft. Drain, but save the water. It makes a fantastic start to a vegetable stock. Put the drained cloves back in the pot. Add the ice and cover with water. When the cloves have cooled, drain thoroughly.

You can freeze these, so do a bunch.

CARAMELIZED ONIONS

Caramelized onions are so good. Try spoonfuls of them with sour cream on a steak . . . or add them to just about anything you are cooking for a deep, sweet flavor. If you are trying to sell your house, make these. Your house will smell like the most wonderful, homey place in the world.

MAKES 2 CUPS/420 G

---

8 cups/1041 g onions, sliced
1 cup/235 ml vegetable oil
1 bay leaf

Preheat your oven to 325°F/163°C. In a 9 x 12-inch/23 cm x 30 cm oven-safe casserole, stir the onions with the oil. They should be about 1½ inches/4 cm deep. Tuck the bay leaf into the onions. Put it in the oven. Now be patient. Check every 15 minutes, stirring to keep the browning even. Your onions need to be totally soft, and somewhat brown. Keep going. This may take an hour and a half. It's worth it. Besides, the oven is doing most of the work.

Let cool and refrigerate. While they're sitting on your counter, try dipping some focaccia into the onion oil. Mmmm.

The onions will keep for a week, and you can freeze them.

ROASTED RED PEPPERS

As usual, this is a cheater method, rather than one of the many complicated and time consuming ways to roast peppers that cooks like to argue over. We essentially fry-roast them in the oven. Make as many as you can; they are a good thing to have around to add to salads or pizza, serve next to meat or blend into a salad dressing. You can use the same method for any peppers you want to roast.

MAKES ½ CUP/260 G

2 red sweet peppers
Olive oil
Salt
Coarsely ground black pepper

Preheat your oven to 450°F/232°C.

Seed the peppers and rip them up into 1-inch/2.5 cm pieces. Toss in olive oil to coat and season them with salt and pepper. Spread out in an oven-safe casserole that accommodates a single layer of peppers.

Put the pan in the oven. We aren't going to peel these, because what a pain. That means you need to keep a close eye on how fast they are cooking. You want them cooked through and charred just a bit. Any more than that and the skins will get bitter and brittle. This should take 8 minutes or less.

Let cool to room temperature and refrigerate, covered with olive oil.

AIOLI

This garlicky aioli is a vast improvement on store-bought mayonnaise. Use it on sandwiches, to make crab or lobster or tuna salad, to dip your French fries into. The eggs are not cooked, so use good fresh ones or buy pasteurized eggs.

MAKES ABOUT ¾ CUP/177 ML

2 large egg yolks
3 to 4 cloves garlic
1 tsp freshly squeezed lemon juice
½ cup/120 ml good olive oil or a neutral vegetable oil

Place the egg yolks, garlic and lemon juice in a blender. Blend until smooth. With the blender running, slowly pour in the oil. Blend until emulsified. This will keep for weeks in your refrigerator.

CHEATER AIOLI

The regular Aioli is so easy that this isn't much of a time-saver, but it does avoid the use of raw eggs and you don't have to dirty a blender. It still beats regular mayonnaise! This recipe makes a single serving; scale up as needed

MAKES A SCANT ¼ CUP/60 ML

3 tbsp/46 ml mayonnaise
1 tsp/3 g garlic, minced
¼ tsp freshly squeezed lemon juice

Mix it all together. Keep it for ages.

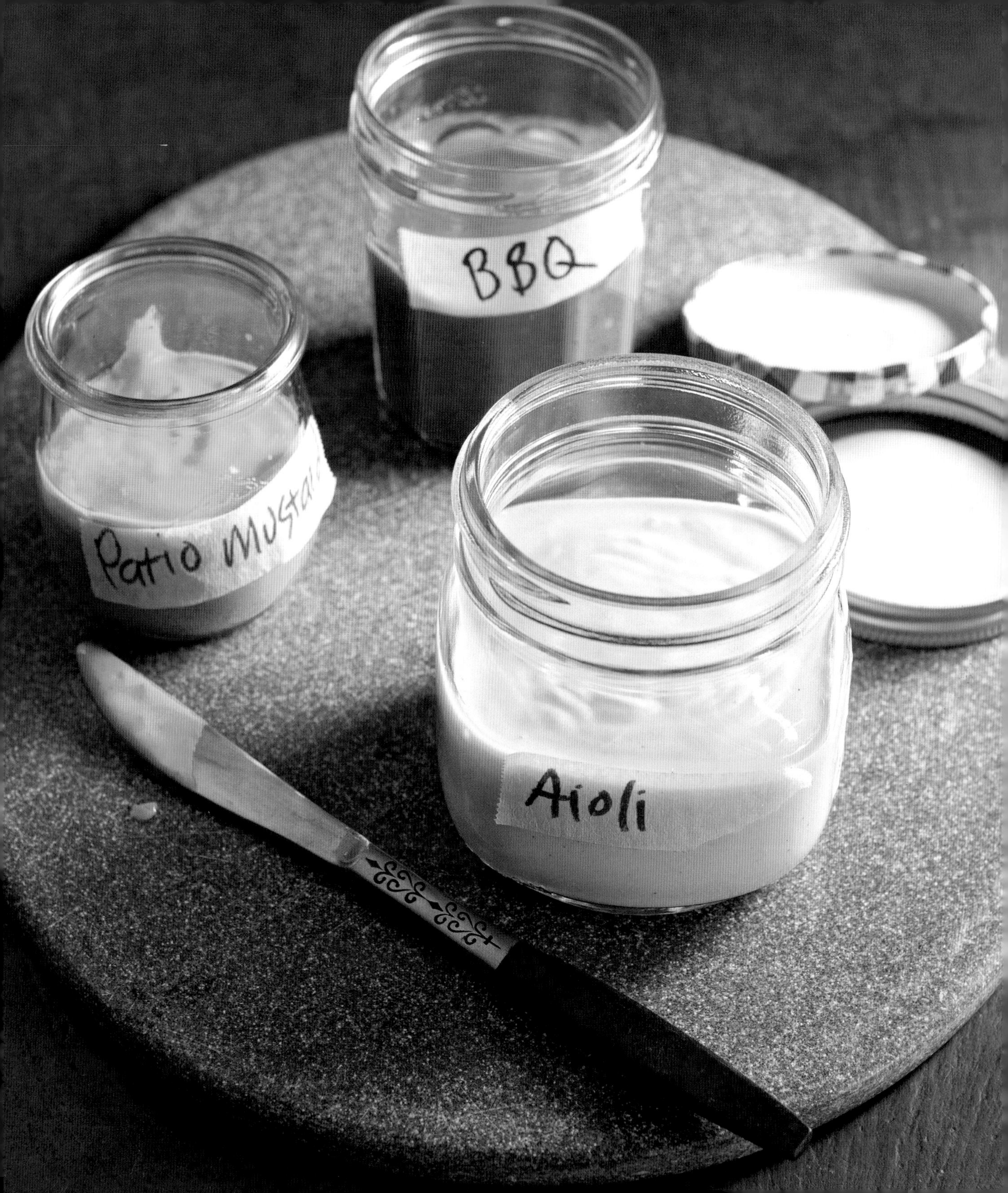
BBQ
Patio Mustard
Aioli

JAY H'S BARBECUE SAUCE

Jay H was an employee long ago; now he's a lobsterman, snowboarder, friend and spouse of a current employee. It's hard to get away, I tell you. Back in the '90s, before the BBQ explosion, he and I agreed that we were dissatisfied with the sauces that were available commercially. This is the one we came up with. It's easy as H-E-double-hockey-sticks.

MAKES ABOUT 2½ CUPS/591 ML

2 tbsp/30 ml extra-virgin olive oil

2 tbsp/30 ml Worcestershire sauce (use the Lea & Perrins, not the generic crap)

2 tbsp/30 ml water

2 tbsp/14 g dried onion flakes

4 cloves garlic

1 cup/237 ml canned whole tomatoes in juice

1 tsp red pepper flakes

1 tbsp/8 g chili powder

1¼ tsp/3 g coarsely ground black pepper

2 tbsp/30 ml white vinegar

2 tbsp/30 ml prepared mustard

⅔ tsp salt

¼ cup/60 ml molasses

Oh, this is hard: Blend. Keeps as long as Keith Richards.

PATIO MUSTARD

For a while, some time ago, I had a hot-dog cart on the patio at Cafe Miranda. This mustard was our standard out there, so it became Patio Mustard. It will be good on your patio, too. It's an attempt to reproduce a Caribbean-style mustard that was once brought to me by one of my mentors, the late Robert Baynes, and his wife, Deanna. I use a regular, cheap mustard and gussy it up with spicy Sriracha, lime juice, a little sweetener and a bunch of cilantro.

MAKES 2⅔ CUPS/621 ML

¼ cup/60 ml Sriracha

2 tbsp/30 ml freshly squeezed lime juice

2 tbsp/30 ml light corn syrup

¼ cup fresh cilantro (stems are OK)

2 cups cheap yellow mustard

Put everything but the mustard in the blender. BUZZZZZZZZZZZZ. (In other words, puree until smooth.) Mix well into the mustard.

Keeps for ages.

Use in: Pork Mole (page 128), Meat Loaf and Potatoes Dinner (page 135), pHd Hot Dog (page 183), Reuben's Long-Lost Cousin (page 181), NASCAR Pâté (page 194), with knockwurst or kielbasa or with black beans and rice.

SALSA EVELYN

This is a fresh-tasting, bright-flavored salsa that is great with tortilla chips or as a condiment with Mexican-type food. It can also be used as a cooking sauce for fish or chicken. Make a seafood gazpacho by adding cucumbers, fish stock, crab or lobster and a dollop of sour cream. The possibilities are endless.

MAKES 4 CUPS/946 ML

28 oz/796 g of your favorite canned whole tomatoes
4 to 5 sprigs cilantro
2 canned chipotle peppers
1 tbsp/15 ml adobo sauce from the chipotle can
2 cloves garlic
Salt
Coarsely ground black pepper
Juice from 1 lime
1½ tbsp/22 ml good extra-virgin olive oil
6 or 7 coriander seeds

Drain the tomatoes, reserving the liquid. Put everything but the tomatoes in the food processor with the tomato liquid. Blitz almost to a puree. Add the tomatoes and pulse to chop.

Keep it in the refrigerator for 2 weeks.

SECRET SPICE

This spice is magic. The idea is similar to curry powder, but without some of the more floral cinnamon-ish notes that you'll find in a garam masala or similar blends. Another difference is the toasting process. Traditionally, spices are bloomed in oil to bring out their full flavor. Because this one gets bloomed in the oven instead, you can sprinkle it right on your food.

Full disclosure: This is really only Semi-Secret Spice. At the restaurant, the ingredients list is much longer and would scare people away (plus, there are some secrets I want to keep). This version is a shortcut that uses commercial curry powder as a base. It is much easier, and will make whatever you put it on much more delicious.

MAKES 1⅓ CUPS/ 139 G

1 cup/100 g curry powder
¼ cup/28 g paprika
1 tsp cayenne pepper
1 tsp ground coriander
1 tsp ground cumin
2 tsp/5 g finely ground black or white pepper

Preheat your oven to 175°F/79°C.

Mix the spices together and spread to a thickness of ¼ inch/ 6 mm on a cookie sheet. Toast for 45 minutes.

Use in: Secret Scallops (page 145), Lamb and Veg Wowie (page 139), Wontons from Spaaaace (page 30), Gnu Thing (page 142) and anything that could use a sprinkle of magic.

ACKNOWLEDGMENTS

I don't want to give a bad Oscar speech, but there are a lot of people who supported, inspired and contributed to the creation of this book and the restaurant that it represents. I just hope I don't leave anyone out (and my mascara doesn't run).

This book would never have happened without the stupendous efforts and talents of my cowriter, Kate Gaudet, and photographer, Stacey Cramp. Jeff Gnecco—Kate's husband, my lawyer and my friend—got the whole process going. Will Kiester at Page Street Publishing gave us a chance to make this idea a reality. Melissa Kelly offered her encouragement from the beginning and wrote a foreword that brings tears to my eyes, and it is not because I am cutting onions.

The recipes here stand on the shoulders of the giants I learned to cook from, starting with my grandmother, Constance Altiero. Anthony M. Casasanto and C. Barry Maron, Brian Morell, Joe Lotozo and the late Tim Watts employed, hazed, indoctrinated and encouraged me as a young cook.

I cannot give a big enough thanks to the Krue at Cafe Miranda, now headed by Chef Andrew Hansen along with Amanda Duckworth. The kitchen and house teams of past and present have put their hearts, minds and energy into the restaurant every day. There would be no Miranda without them.

It takes a village to run a restaurant, and I have to thank all the wonderful professionals who contributed their expertise as well as their goodwill over the years. Among them are Renee Philbrook, Farmer Anne Perkins, Victoria Condon and Eric Belley, who all turned out to be good friends as well as business associates. Kathryn Langston, Deanna Riggin Smith and the late Bob Baynes, Cathy Madaffari and Arthur Hernandez, William Donnelly, Suzy Ellis and Chris Ellis provided substantial support. I am grateful to the town of Rockland and its past and present public servants, starting with Bob Peabody and Dake Collins. I thank the fire and police departments for being there for us when we needed them.

Evelyn Donnelly cofounded Cafe Miranda with me, and I thank her for many years of partnership.

Our customers, from Rockland and away, are the life and breath of Cafe Miranda, from the locals whom we see every week to the thousands from across the country and around the world who come back year after year.

The recipes in this book were tested for home use by some fabulous cooks across the country and the globe: Erin Bagley, Joanne Billington, Lisa Breheney, Mike and Margaret Burman, Lisa Collins, Lindsay and Mike DiCuirci, Julia Gaudet, Tom Perrin and Elizabeth Hutcheon, Francesca Ritter and especially E. J. Gaudet. Thank you for your efforts and your helpful advice.

Finally, I have to thank the family and friends who have stood by me through thick and thin. My son, Evan Altiero, makes me prouder every day. Love and thanks to Carl Altiero and his family, Florence Altiero Madaffari and her family, the late Keith Altiero, the Duckworth clan, Mike Baron, Pepe and Julio Limantour, Kristina Rowe, Miranda A. Dawg, Miloh D. Dawg and all the Skooks who are close to my heart.

INDEX